theology

TH1NK REFERENCE COLLECTION

theology

THINK FOR YOURSELF ABOUT WHAT YOU BELIEVE

Written by General Editor Mark Tabb

TH1NK
P.O. Box 35001
Colorado Springs, Colorado 80935

TH1NK is an imprint of NavPress.

TH1NK and the TH1NK logo are registered trademarks of NavPress. Absence of ® in connection with marks of NavPress or other parties does not indicate an absence of registration of those marks.

ISBN 1-57683-957-5

Cover design by Arvid Wallen
Creative Team: Nicci Hubert, Karen Lee-Thorp, Erika Hueneke, Kathy Mosier, Bob Bubnis

Tabb, Mark A.
 Theology : think for yourself about what you believe / written by Mark Tabb.
    p. cm. -- (TH1NK reference collection)
 Includes bibliographical references.
 ISBN 1-57683-957-5
 1. Theology, Doctrinal--Popular works. I. Title. II. Series.
 BT77.T28 2006
 230--dc22
                          2006013491
Printed in the United States of America

1 2 3 4 5 6 7 8 9 10 / 10 09 08 07 06

To David Dockery,
who introduced me to the wonders of theology and the
joy of thinking for myself about what I believe

Contents

About the TH1NK
REFERENCE COLLECTION

The TH1NK REFERENCE COLLECTION isn't an ordinary set of reference books. Like all of the books in the TH1NK line, we wrote these books for students. That doesn't mean we inserted some hip language into an otherwise dry, boring book to try to make it sound with it and cool, dude. Instead, we built these books on a couple of assumptions about you.

First, we knew you want honest representations of various points of view. Although all the books in the REFERENCE COLLECTION are written from an evangelical Christian position, we didn't dismiss all other viewpoints. Instead, we wrote these books in such a way that those holding different worldviews and theological perspectives would be able to read these books and say, *Yes, this gives a good outline of what I and others believe.* To assure theological balance, all of the books in this collection have been reviewed by a panel of scholars from various theological perspectives and academic fields (see page 283 for a list of those scholars).

We also believed you are able to draw your own conclusions. Whether the question regards what Buddhists believe or whether Christians can lose their salvation, we didn't connect all the dots for you. Each book presents several perspectives. You will have to take the next step on your own and figure out what you believe and why you believe it. Our goal is to do more than answer questions. The TH1NK REFERENCE COLLECTION is designed to make you think through your own beliefs and convictions, as well as those of others.

Finally, we assumed you want something more than a place to turn for answers to your questions about Islam or Psalm 119 or the role of women in the church. That's why we designed these books to be read, not just used for research. You can read them from cover to cover. Along the way, you will find that these books not only dispense information but also entertain you and challenge you and the way you see your world.

Mark Tabb
General Editor

Introduction

Consequently, if you do not listen to Theology,
that will not mean that you have no ideas about God.
It will mean you have a lot of wrong ones.
C. S. LEWIS

What you believe matters. It may well be the only thing that matters. Your beliefs shape your every decision, from what you had for breakfast this morning to your career path to whether or not you choose to get married and have children. Every choice you make is largely determined by the ideas rolling around in your head. All those facts you know to be true, along with everything you think might be true and all that stuff you hope isn't true, have conspired together to make you who you are. Ideas are the single most powerful force in the world, and along the way, you've put together an odd assortment of them that have shaped you. As you continue to add to that collection, your life will evolve. You determine your future today by the beliefs you decide to hold on to, as well as those you choose to reject as false.

This is especially true of your theology — that is, your beliefs about God. The word *theology* means the study or science of God, just as *biology* is the study of life, and *sociology* is the study of social institutions and relationships. Grouping these together may sound strange to postmodern ears, but that hasn't always been the case. In the Middle Ages, theology was known as "The Queen of the Sciences," for it was the unifying principle that drove the study of every other area of life. We usually think of science and theology as fighting against one another, but the scientific revolution was born out of a Christian worldview. Francis Bacon, Isaac Newton, Blaise Pascal, Louis Pasteur, and many other early heroes of science all professed faith in Christ. They believed a reasonable God created the universe. That, in their minds, made scientific discovery possible. Their beliefs about God both drove them to the sciences and worked as the filter through which they interpreted their research.

In the same way, your theology shapes everything else you believe, even if your theology leaves no room for God. That's why cosmonaut Gherman Titov, the second man to orbit the earth, looked out the window of his *Vostok II* spacecraft as he hurtled through space and said, "I am high in the sky, and still I do not see the face of God."[1] Yet King David, staring up at a night sky three thousand years earlier, said, "The heavens declare the glory of God" (Psalm 19:1, NIV). How could both men, looking at the same sky, albeit one with a better view than the other, reach such different conclusions? Titov believed God wasn't there, while David knew he was.

Because your theology influences every other part of your life, you not only need to know what you believe about God, but you also need to think through those beliefs. Few people ever do that. Most of us walk through life collecting beliefs like my youngest daughter chooses socks each morning. She reaches into a drawer and grabs whatever her hand finds first. The colors don't matter. Wearing a green and red Christmas sock along with an orange and black jack-o'-lantern Halloween sock in the middle of April doesn't bother her at all. If it will slip between her foot and her Chuck Taylors, she will wear it. That's how most people put on their ideas about God. They grab an idea from a verse they read in the Bible in the morning, along with something they heard on *Oprah* in the afternoon, and combine them with a thought a friend said in an IM conversation. But they rarely, if ever, stand back and look at how all their ideas go together, or how those ideas line up with what God says about himself.

That's not the worst of it. Many people, maybe even most people, never look ahead to see where their odd collection of beliefs and ideas will take them. They never consider the long-term consequences or the logical outcome of what they believe to be true. This isn't a new phenomenon. One hundred years ago G. K. Chesterton wrote:

> At any innocent tea-table we may easily hear a man say, "Life is not worth living." We regard it as we regard the statement that it is a fine day; nobody thinks that it can possibly have any serious effect on the man or on the world. And yet if that utterance were really believed, the world would stand on its head. Murderers would be given medals for saving men from life; firemen would be denounced for keeping men from death; poisons would be used as medicines; doctors would be called in when people were well; the Royal Humane Society would be rooted out like a horde of assassins. Yet we never speculate as to whether the conversational pessimist will strengthen or disorganize society; for we are convinced that theories do not matter.[2]

But theories do matter, because your beliefs matter. That's where this book comes in. It's designed to make you think seriously about your own theology. We want you to examine what you say you believe when you claim to be a Christian, why you believe it, and how those beliefs will express themselves in your life when you consistently live them. You won't find easy answers couched in religious clichés in these pages. Easy answers don't fare too well when you sit down in a classroom and everything you ever believed is called into question. Reciting clichés in the face of credible arguments from other worldviews makes as much sense as saying alligators are ornery because they have so many teeth and no toothbrush. You need something more if your faith is to survive as it brushes up against the real world. Nor will you grow up in your faith the way God desires if we tell you what you should think. Spiritual maturity comes as you learn to think biblically. That is the ultimate goal of this book. We want to help you be mature and full grown in the Lord, measuring up to the full stature of Christ. Then we will no longer be like children, forever changing our minds about what we believe because someone has told us something different or because someone has cleverly lied to us and made the lie sound like the truth. Instead, we will hold to the truth in love, becoming more and more in every way like Christ, who is the head of his body, the church. (Ephesians 4:13-15)

Black and White and Shades of Gray

We live in a pluralistic culture where tolerance is the supreme virtue, but the Bible doesn't share that sensitivity. It makes bold statements couched in absolute terms that leave no room for competing ideas. Deuteronomy 4:39 says, "The LORD is God both in heaven and on earth, and there is no other god!" Jesus echoed Deuteronomy when he said, "I am the way, the truth, and the life. No one can come to the Father except through me" (John 14:6). These statements must be true or false. Either the God of the Bible is the one true God and Jesus is the only Way to this God, or both are liars. They cannot be true for me and not for you, no matter how deeply we may wish otherwise. The Lord refuses to play that game. You don't have to believe these statements are true, but according to the Bible, the consequences of refusing to believe last forever.

However, not everything in the Bible and Christian theology is as cut-and-dried as Deuteronomy 4:39. The Bible boldly declares that Jesus died, rose again bodily, and ascended into heaven. It also says he will return to earth some day to take control of God's kingdom once and for all. Yet in the Bible, a lot of the details of Jesus' second coming are hazy. Questions abound as to whether he will return to rule on earth for a thousand years before the eternal age is ushered in, or if he will come after Christians have established his reign on earth for a thousand years, or whether all the references to Christ's thousand-year reign are to be taken metaphorically. Even those who agree on the first scenario disagree as to the details of how and when Christ's reign will come, and how his return relates to a time of trouble called the Great Tribulation.

In the same way, Christians don't always see eye to eye on theological issues such as baptism, the role of women in the church, speaking in tongues, the age of the earth, and whether it's possible to lose your salvation, just to name a few. Christianity may be a religion of the Book, but not everyone agrees on which translation of the Bible should be used. There's even disagreement over whether a Christ follower should dance, play cards, or have a glass of wine with dinner. While these questions don't determine whether a person will spend eternity in heaven or in hell, disagreements over them have caused more than one person to wonder why Christians can't get along.

The fact that everything in the Bible isn't crystal clear surprises most newcomers to the faith. They wonder why God would leave anything in his Word open to interpretation by the reader. In response, many people run to one of two extremes. The first is the all-gray group. In this group's view, nothing in the Bible is set in stone. Every idea is fluid. God. Jesus. The Holy Spirit. Who they are and what they do all come down to preferences, not absolutes. Theology is whatever you decide to make it. For the all-gray group, there are no wrong answers.

The second extreme is the there's-no-such-thing-as-gray group. People in this group want to uphold truth and the Bible and absolute standards of morality. Unfortunately, in their zeal to combat the fuzziness of the all-gray group, they make everything black-and-white. Pick an issue, and they have *the* answer. From the music in a worship service to the clothes you wear, the Bible has one, definitive answer. For the there's-no-such-thing-as-gray group, there's no room for compromise, because compromise means falling onto a slippery slope toward relativism.

Further compounding our difficulty is the fact that some of the theological issues people think of as black-and-white aren't so clear in the Bible, and some of the grays appear more distinctive when we actually read what God has to say about them. That's why, for the purposes of this book, the essentials of Christianity are those teachings of the Bible that have generally been agreed upon by followers of Jesus around the world for the past two thousand years. These are the central truths of our faith that believers have given their lives to uphold, the key teachings of both the Old and New Testaments that define what it means to be a Christian. The essentials include the belief that God has spoken with absolute truth, the doctrine of the Trinity, the deity and humanity of Jesus, and his bodily resurrection from the dead. Essentials also include the deity of the Holy Spirit, salvation through faith in Christ alone, and the need for Christian community called the church.

We will also explore the gray areas of Christianity, those issues that have divided believers over the past two thousand years. While some may seem as black-and-white as the print on this page to you, another person reading this book who comes from a different background sees them as anything but. His ideas seem as black-and-white to him as yours do to you. Believe it or not, the theological gray areas play a very important role in God's overall plan for your life. Jesus said the key distinctive of his followers would be the love we have for one another (see John 13:35). Anyone can love those who are just like him, but it's hard for people to get along with others whose ideas clash with theirs, much less love them. These gray areas allow us to put into practice Paul's words to the church in Rome:

> Welcome with open arms fellow believers who don't see things the way you do. And don't jump all over them every time they do or say something you don't agree with — even when it seems that they are strong on opinions but weak in the faith department. Remember, they have their own history to deal with. Treat them gently. (Romans 14:1, MSG)

Diversity within the Christian family also fits the pattern we see in the rest of God's creation. God loves variety. Why else would he make somewhere between two hundred and four hundred breeds of dog?[3] Only God could dream up a way to have ten-pound miniature dachshunds and 130-pound mastiffs come out of the same genetic stock. It shouldn't surprise us then to find such variety within the Christian faith. If God had wanted every believer to be a hymn-singing, organ-playing, loud-sermon-preaching Baptist, he would have made sure every church fit that profile. Since it's hard to find two Baptists who are exactly alike, much less fit Presbyterians, Catholics, and Pentecostals into a single box, we must conclude that God finds pleasure in the diversity within his family. This isn't meant to imply that every group that calls itself Christian is actually part of God's family. Many cults, such as the Mormons and the Jehovah's Witnesses who deny the essentials of the faith, try to portray themselves as followers of Jesus. Their claims only underscore the importance of understanding biblical theology.

Saying God finds pleasure in diversity also doesn't mean that the doctrinal differences between denominations don't matter or that questions concerning these differences don't have a right or wrong answer. Beliefs matter, because they will determine your approach to the entire Christian life. Not all of the answers believers have come up with to the questions over which Christians disagree are correct. When Jesus returns, the question of the relationship between his return and his thousand-year reign, as well as every other theological question, will be settled once and for all. But until then, differences of opinion over baptism or tongues or the role of women within the church shouldn't distract us from the work Jesus gave us to complete while we await his return. Nor should they cause us to turn our attention to fighting against one another while a lost world slips further and further away from God.

That is the purpose of this book. We want to help ground you in the essentials while opening your eyes to the possibility that there's room in God's family for more than one approach to the nonessentials. That also explains why this book doesn't contain a definitive answer on the gray areas. We called this *Think for Yourself About What You Believe* for a reason. Even in those areas that are essential to the Christian faith, we want you to think about how your life should change if these ideas are true, as well as what you should do if they are not.

Your beliefs set the course of your life. Therefore, you need to look ahead and see where the essential truths of Christianity will ultimately take you. God's truth will not leave you unchanged. The ideas he wants to implant inside you through his Word will change the course of your life. You also need to ponder how your life should change if these truths turn out to be nothing but legends. Then, you need to step back and ask yourself which of these two paths you are already walking down. Does your life reflect the growing influence of God's eternal truths? Or do you live like God and his Word are nothing but noise, even as you say you believe in him?

We also want you to think through the gray areas of the faith. We present multiple views on the questions about which believers disagree. But we don't tell you which view is right and which is wrong. That is by design. We want you to examine the issues involved. Listen to what the Bible has to say. Then think. Your future depends on it.

1

God Has Spoken

ESSENTIALS

General Revelation: God has revealed himself through his works to show us that he is real.

Special Revelation: God has revealed himself through his Word, the Bible, so that we might know him personally.

QUESTIONS

Which Bible is the right Bible?

Can the Bible ever be wrong?

There is a God, and he has spoken. That is the basic starting point for the Christian faith. Everything we believe as followers of Jesus hangs on the truth that God exists and he has spoken. This statement is also the Christian response to what Jean-Paul Sartre called the basic philosophical question: Why is there something rather than nothing? There is something because God spoke. Genesis opens with the line, "In the beginning God . . ." His existence isn't explained; he is simply assumed. Before there was anything else, God was there. Then God shattered the silence of nothingness and spoke all of creation into existence. If God did not exist, nothing else would either. And if God had remained silent, the universe would never have sprung into existence.

God spoke every created thing into existence with one exception: you and me. The Bible says he shaped the first man and woman in his own image. The moment he finished, he started up a conversation with them. He gave them a few simple guidelines to lead them in their lives on this new world. Sadly, the first man and woman chose to ignore God, but that wasn't the end of his conversation with the human race. He kept on talking, and he continues to speak today. Because God *is*, he speaks to those he made like himself. As Hebrews 1:1-2 tells us, "Long ago God spoke many times and in many ways to our ancestors through the prophets. But now in these final days, he has spoken to us through his Son."

ESSENTIALS

General Revelation: God has revealed himself through his works to show us that he is real.

"God exists and he has spoken" is more than a religious statement. Christianity stands or falls on whether or not there really is a God and whether or not he truly has communicated with the human race in very specific ways. At this point, most books like this rattle off a list of proofs for God's existence, yet the Bible itself never does this. God is the one constant throughout all sixty-six books, yet none of the books contains a systematic list of answers to all the skeptics' questions. Even in Genesis, God's existence isn't explained in any way. That doesn't mean we're left to accept God on blind faith without any evidence whatsoever. From the beginning of time, God has demonstrated who he is through what he does. His fingerprints on his works make the case for God even before we open his special revelation of himself in the Bible.

Think about it this way: When Michael Crichton writes a story, who he is permeates every part of it. Within each novel he creates worlds where dinosaurs are cloned from drops of blood found in fossilized mosquitoes, or where free-floating nanoparticles take on human forms and wreak havoc on those who try to stop them. The worlds he creates reflect the unique person who is Michael Crichton, including the words he uses, the plots he spins—even the characters he invents to populate his worlds. After reading *The Andromeda Strain* and *The Lost World*, you don't even need to see his name on the cover to know he wrote *State of Fear*. The first few pages give him away. In the same way, Dr. Seuss's books share a distinctive style, yet they also sound nothing like anything created by any other writer, unless of course that writer is trying to imitate Seuss. Growing up on a steady diet of *Hop on Pop* and *The Cat in the Hat*, you would never confuse Theodor Geisel with the author of *Jurassic Park*. Nor would you think Crichton wrote *Green Eggs and Ham.* The two men's styles are too different, and their books show it.

Books reflect their authors. They can't avoid it. God's works do the same thing. Theologians call this *general revelation*—that is, God's revealing of himself, his power and divinity, to all people at all times and places. Also called natural revelation, this is the way God speaks without words through creation, history, and human nature. Although general revelation doesn't communicate enough about God for a person to enter into a personal relationship with him, it does tell those who pay attention that he exists, that he is powerful, and that he is a God of order, artistry, and purpose. God's voice through his works leaves people without an excuse when they claim they knew nothing of him (see Romans 1:19-20).

Fingerprints on Creation

God speaking through creation or the natural world means that when we look up at the stars or gaze at a California hill covered with wildflowers, we see the fingerprints of God. The more we fix our eyes on the wonder of creation, the more we must conclude that these things could not make themselves. Both the intricate design of creation and the way the universe appears to be fine-tuned for life declare that this couldn't happen by chance. Consider the following: If the electromagnetic force in atoms were weakened by a mere 4 percent, then the sun would immediately explode (the diproton would have a bound state, which would increase the solar luminosity by a factor 10^{18}). If it were stronger, there would be fewer stable atoms. If the protons were 0.2 percent heavier, they would decay into neutrons unable to hold on to electrons, so there would be no stable atoms around. If the proton-to-electron mass ratio were much smaller, there could be no stable stars, and if it were much larger, there could be no ordered structures such as crystals and DNA molecules.[1]

God doesn't just speak through the order and design we find in creation, but also through the jaw-dropping beauty that surrounds us. From something as mundane as a group of bright red cardinals sitting in a leaf-bare bush on a snowy Midwestern day, to the spectacular views of nebulae in distant corners of the galaxy beamed to earth by the Hubble Space Telescope,[2] creation doesn't just tell us that a Creator exists, but that this Creator is an artist without peer. The feelings of awe that come over us as we watch the waves pound against the rocks at the beach or hold a newborn baby for the first time are in fact God speaking to us through his masterpiece. Psalm 19:1-4 puts it this way:

> The heavens declare the glory of God;
>> the skies proclaim the work of his hands.
> Day after day they pour forth speech;
>> night after night they display knowledge.
> There is no speech or language
>> where their voice is not heard.
> Their voice goes out into all the earth,
>> their words to the ends of the world. (NIV)

While the order and beauty of the universe appear to be rock-solid proofs of God's existence to believers, unbelievers find many ways to explain them away. Physicist Max Tegmark writes extensively on the way our universe is fine-tuned for life, yet he doesn't see this fine-tuning as evidence of a Creator. Rather, he sees it as further proof of the existence of parallel universes where such fine-tuning does not exist and life is not possible. For him, the fact that we find ourselves in a universe teeming with life is no more of a miracle than checking into a hotel and being given a room with the same number as the year of your birth. Room 1985 exists because all the other rooms exist. In the same way, Tegmark believes an infinite number of universes exist where every possible combination of physical laws rule. Some have life while others cannot.[3] Other scientists regard what we call beauty as nothing more than the end result of natural selection playing out over eons of time. Bright red cardinals sit in bushes on snowy days because red feathers made the males of the species more attractive to the females. That's why this trait became dominant in cardinals—no further reason. For those who see the hand of natural selection in the world rather than the fingerprints of God, beauty is purely in the eyes of the beholder. Believers may hear God's revelation of himself through nature, but clearly, not everyone is listening.

Fingerprints on History

If God speaks through his works, then we should be able to see his hand not only in the created universe, but also in the way the history of that universe plays out over time. This is the second method of general revelation. The Bible says God started history when he created the heavens and the earth and that he will bring it to a close when Jesus returns. In between, believers see the invisible hand of God guiding the ebb and flow of historical events to accomplish God's greater purposes. This doesn't mean that God finds pleasure in everything that takes place on the world stage, but rather that God directs the larger picture of history to move the human race toward his ultimate goal.

For many believers, no event demonstrates the hand of God in history more than the survival of the Jewish people. The Jews trace their lineage to Abraham, whom God promised to make into a great people through whom the entire world would be blessed. When God first made this promise, Abraham and his wife, Sarah, were old and childless. Yet they believed God, and he made good on his promise. Throughout history numerous groups have tried to exterminate the Jews, most recently Nazi Germany during the Holocaust. Yet not only have the Jews survived — they've thrived. In 1948, they once again took possession of the land God promised Abraham nearly two thousand years before Christ. The fact that Abraham's descendants could survive as a distinct people for so long in spite of the horrendous travails they've endured is evidence that something more than the blind hand of history is at play here. God must be involved, as he makes sure the people he chose so long ago continue to bear witness to who he is. The survival of the Jews is but one historical reality that Christians point to as evidence of God's hand in history.

However, before we leap to too many conclusions, we need to keep in mind that interpreting history is a subjective exercise. Prior to the outbreak of the First World War, the German people were told "Providence" had selected them to occupy the supreme place in the history of the universe.[4] Obviously, history showed it had something else in mind entirely. In the same way, the arguments that are used to prove that God has preserved the Jewish race throughout history could also be used to prove that Fidel Castro rules Cuba by divine command and that the Mormons' trek through the desert in the mid-1800s makes them God's New World equivalent of the Israelites. Most evangelical believers would never make those leaps. That's why history falls under the umbrella of *general* revelation. Although God may well speak through history, his message isn't exactly crystal clear.

Fingerprints on the Soul

People crave purpose.[5] They want their lives to have meaning. Deep down inside our souls, we long to find the reason for our existence. This quest for meaning permeates every form of human expression, from art to music to literature. Yet if God doesn't exist, intrinsic meaning is an illusion. If everything, including human beings, is nothing more than the end result of time plus chance, then the physical universe is basically an accident. Some master plan doesn't rule the flow of events through time. Life just *is*. Without a God with a divine plan for each life, human beings simply live and die. There is no greater purpose. There is no eternal reason for your life. Your life is whatever you make it, and once it's over, it's over.

Yet human beings are repulsed by the idea of life without meaning or ultimate worth. Such thoughts lead to depression or something far worse. French painter Paul Gauguin (1848–1903) tried to convey this sense of despair over the meaninglessness of life in his painting *Where Do We Come From? What Are We? Where Are We Going?* Prior to painting his masterpiece, he had deserted his family and tried to find the answers to life's ultimate questions by living with the "noble savages" of Tahiti. Yet in the end, he concluded that there are no answers. Life is nothing more than a cruel dance that ends in death. He put his conclusions on canvas. After he finished painting the picture, he tried to commit suicide, although he failed.[6] Gauguin's suicide attempt was not an act of madness, but the only sane act in a world devoid of meaning. If life has no point, what is the point in living?

Christian theology understands this craving within the human soul to be a sign of God's fingerprint on those he made in his image. In the book of Ecclesiastes, King Solomon explored this quest for meaning and the impossibility of finding it apart from God. Human beings can't help but long for something more out of life than what can be experienced through the five senses, because, in the words of Solomon, "[God] has planted eternity in the human heart, but even so, people cannot see the whole scope of God's work from beginning to end" (Ecclesiastes 3:11).

People not only crave meaning; they also have an intrinsic sense of right and wrong and a longing for justice. C. S. Lewis called this the "natural law," or rules of decent behavior.[7] Even critics who say rules of right and wrong are matters of taste, not absolutes, must agree that no one can live without them. Put another way, if right and wrong are illusions, then there is no real moral difference between helping a little old lady across the street and shoving her in front of a bus. No one in his right mind would agree with that statement, and even if he tried, he wouldn't be able to live out its implications consistently. Any society based on such a convoluted sense of morality would disintegrate and soon cease to exist. Why? Christianity says the reason lies in the way God made human beings. He made us in his image, and something about that image keeps calling us back to him, no matter how hard we try to drown out the voice.

The truly fascinating aspect of the natural law is the fact that no one consistently keeps it. We may not shove little old ladies in front of buses, but we violate basic moral standards we know everyone should keep. Lewis saw this as proof of the divine origin of the natural law. Everyone says, "Well, no one is perfect," yet if this natural law was nothing more than a human creation, why would we set the bar so high that no one can attain it? Something—or Someone—else must be in play here, and that Someone is God. Not only has he written his law in a book called the Bible; he has also etched it on human hearts (see Romans 2:14-15). We know what we should do, even when we don't do it.

As with the other expressions of general revelation, not everyone agrees with this conclusion. A naturalist—that is, one who believes the physical universe is all there is and all there ever will be—believes society's agreed-upon rules of right and wrong evolved along with human beings as a way of ensuring our survival. The moral difference between helping a little old lady across the street and shoving her in front of a bus comes not by divine revelation, but by the imprint of social norms attained through thousands of years of evolution. Cultures that showed little respect for life did not survive, while those that respected life flourished. That explains why one is the norm and not the other. In the eyes of those who don't believe in a God who gives moral absolutes, helping others rather than harming them is morally superior because it's more expedient to the survival of the species—nothing more.

Thus, while general revelation points to an eternal God who created the universe and actively involves himself in it, nothing revealed in this way enforces belief in God. Those who prefer other explanations can construct them. But for those who are willing to see them, God's fingerprints cover his works just as the personality of an author flows through his books. If God is, and if he has spoken, then the evidence surrounds us.

But this is only the beginning of the story. God's voice through creation, history, and the human heart only opens the door for us to listen to his specific message awaiting us in his written Word, the Bible.

Special Revelation: God has revealed himself through his Word, the Bible, so that we might know him personally.

General revelation tells us that God exists. However, if that were all we had to go on, we would never know who this God is. That's where God's special revelation comes in. Special revelation is "God's manifestation of himself to particular persons at definite times and places, enabling those persons to enter into a redemptive relationship with him."[8] Through it God steps out from behind the curtain and tells us not only what he is like, but more importantly, how we can know him personally and intimately.

The Need for Special Revelation

Special revelation makes knowing God possible. The difference between God and human beings is so great that our finite minds cannot comprehend an infinite God unless he himself explains himself to us. In comparison to God, a person is like an amoeba sitting atop the Empire State Building. From the beginning of our existence, we've struggled to comprehend the nature of the physical universe that envelops us, yet the Bible says God measured out the vastness of space with his fingers (see Isaiah 40:12). Obviously, God doesn't have physical hands, but Isaiah uses this analogy to show how God is far greater than our minds can image. If we can't fully comprehend the universe, how much harder will it be for us to figure out the One who designed it?

The limitations of the human mind in relation to God are further complicated by the separation that now exists between God and us, a separation caused by our sin. Romans 1:21 tells us sin has left our minds dark and confused. As a result, human wisdom will never lead anyone to God (see 1 Corinthians 1:21). In its natural state, the human mind cannot understand God's truths. They all sound like nothing but foolishness (see 1 Corinthians 2:14). Unless God spoke up, we would never find him on our own. We would be left groping in the dark, feeling our way toward God in a celestial game of hide-and-seek.

The Nature of Special Revelation

God is a personal God, and his revelation of himself reflects this. Through it he shows us exactly who he is and what he's like. When God revealed himself to Moses in the burning bush, he identified himself by name. "I AM THE ONE WHO ALWAYS IS," he said. "Just tell them, 'I AM has sent me to you'" (Exodus 3:14). Giving his name does more than identify this God in a pantheon of gods. His name, and his revelation of himself, show us who he is.

When he decided to reveal himself to people, God didn't just drop a load of facts about himself down from heaven like statistics on the back of a baseball card. His revelation does much more. The Bible tells us, "God is love" (1 John 4:8). As he interacts with human beings, we learn what this really means. He told Isaiah, "Can a mother forget the baby at her breast and have no compassion on the child she has borne? Though she may forget, I will not forget you! See, I have engraved you on the palms of my hands" (Isaiah 49:15-16, NIV). In reading these words, we not only learn more information about God, but we experience him as well. We feel the depths of his love and hear the intensity of his passion. As we do, we find our souls pulled toward the One who loves us with a love that goes beyond our ability to understand.

Although God's revelation is personal, it doesn't stop there. As he reveals himself, God reveals eternal truth. Jesus himself said to his Father, "Your word is truth" (John 17:17, NIV). Again, our starting point is that God exists, and he has spoken. As he speaks, he reveals both himself and the truth about the world around us. He doesn't just show us himself and leave us to figure out the rest on our own. God's revelation contains the truths upon which our quest for truth in every other field can rest. Given the nature of God, what else would we expect to find? As Hebrews 6:18 says, "It is impossible for God to lie."

Some have tried to downplay this aspect of God's revelation. Twentieth-century theologians such as Emil Brunner maintained that if revelation is regarded as the communication of propositional truths, then faith is nothing more than a mental assent to those truths. The heart is left out. But, according to Brunner, if revelation is regarded as the presentation of a person, then faith is an act of personal trust and commitment to a personal God.[9]

The concerns Brunner and others raise are valid. However, this doesn't have to be an either/or equation. God reveals both himself as a person and eternal truths about himself and his creation. Faith is based upon factual truths, but as we will see in section 5, believing means more than mental assent to information. Jesus' disciples understood the truth that he was indeed the Messiah. They responded to that truth by leaving everything behind to follow him. For them, God's revelation was both informational and personal. That combination proved life changing, both then and now.

Special Revelation and the Bible

Special revelation and the Bible are not synonymous. Revelation is the act by which God shows himself for who he is; the Bible is the written record of this revelation. Not all special revelations are recorded in the Bible, and not everything in the Bible came about through special revelation. Since Jesus was the Son of God, everything he did or said was a special revelation of God his Father. "Anyone who has seen me has seen the Father!" Jesus told his disciples in John 14:9. Yet only a small percentage of Jesus' words and acts are recorded in the Bible. John put it this way: "And I suppose that if all the other things Jesus did were written down, the whole world could not contain the books" (John 21:25). Clearly, not every act of God's special revelation of himself has been preserved.

Nor did everything recorded in the Bible come about through an act of special revelation. When Moses recorded how Pharaoh forced the Israelites to make bricks without supplying them with straw (Exodus 5), he was writing what he observed firsthand. God didn't have to appear to him and show him these events in a miraculous way. As we will see in a moment, God moved Moses' spirit to show him which of these events to include in the book of Exodus, but he didn't have to reveal these events to him.

The Bible also records conversations between people that contain wrong ideas and falsehoods. For example, the book of Job records a long conversation between Job and his friends Eliphaz, Bildad, and Zophar. Although the words of Eliphaz, Bildad, and Zophar are accurately recorded, the things they say are not correct. God himself rebuked Job's comforters in the last chapter of the book, telling them, "I am angry with you and with your two friends, for you have not been right in what you said about me, as my servant Job was" (Job 42:7). These three guys' words may be in the Bible, but they don't reflect God revealing himself to the speakers in a special way.

Preserving God's Revelation: Inspiration

Special revelation is God's act of making himself known to particular persons at definite times and places, enabling those persons to enter into a redemptive relationship with him. Without it, no one would ever come to know God personally. However, because God wanted to make himself known to the entire world, he moved certain people to record his revelation of himself in the Bible. This record includes not only special messages from the Lord (such as the prophets' messages that begin, "This is what the LORD Almighty says"), but also the story of how God worked in the lives of the people to make himself known to the world.

The way God worked in the lives of the Scripture writers to ensure their words were his words is called *inspiration*. This doesn't mean Peter and Paul and the others were inspired by their encounter with God in the same way an artist is inspired by a sunset to paint or a love-struck boy is inspired to write poetry for his beloved. In Christian theology, inspiration refers to the act of the Holy Spirit moving the hearts and minds of the human authors of the Bible so that their words were literally the Word of God.

While this may sound like the Spirit dictated the Bible, that's not what this means. God didn't just use the writers as human tape recorders. When he moved human authors to write his Word, he allowed their unique personalities and perspectives to shine through their writings. Paul's style (Romans–Philemon) is very different from John's (the gospel of John, 1–3 John, Revelation), while both sound nothing like Jeremiah or Malachi. The prayers and praises of the Psalms reflect different perspectives from a different time than the guttural cries for help in Lamentations. The way John described the apocalyptic images of Revelation is very different from Daniel's approach in the book that bears his name. Inspiration, therefore, means that God worked through the totality of each writer: his experiences, his unique perspectives, and the historical situation in which he found himself in the writing of God's Word.

Two passages, 2 Timothy 3:16 and 2 Peter 1:20-21, are most often referred to as explanations of both what inspiration is and how God did it. Second Timothy 3:16 says, "All Scripture is inspired by God and is useful to teach us what is true and to make us realize what is wrong in our lives. It straightens us out and teaches us to do what is right." The Greek word translated "inspired," θεοπνευστος, combines the word θεος, God, with πνεω, to breathe. The term emphasizes the fact that the Bible truly does come from God—he breathed it out. In fact, no stronger Greek word could have been used to emphasize the divine nature of the Bible.[10]

However, θεοπνευστος does not tell us exactly how God moved the writers of the Bible to pen his Word. Second Peter 1:20-21 answers this question. It says, "Above all, you must understand that no prophecy in Scripture ever came from the prophets themselves or because they wanted to prophesy. It was the Holy Spirit who moved the prophets to speak from God." The word translated "moved," φερόμενοι, literally means to pick up and carry. The same term was used to describe carrying a pail of water. That is how the Holy Spirit of God moved those he used to write the Bible. He picked them up and carried them along, opening their minds and moving their spirits to write God's message. The Spirit revealed special messages direct from God and showed which historical events to include in his Word. Part of this carrying along included using the unique life setting into which God placed each writer, as well as their personalities and the experiences they'd lived through before writing the Bible. Again, the Spirit's inspiration didn't come in a vacuum, nor did God simply drop his words down from heaven. The Spirit's carrying of each writer included the totality of the authors' lives (see Jeremiah 1:4-5).

The divine nature of the Scriptures is assumed throughout the Bible. From the Law, to the Prophets and Writings, to the New Testament itself, the Scriptures are referred to as the Word of God. In fact, God and his Word are presented as inseparable. How we treat one reflects our attitude toward the other. John explained, "But those who obey God's word really do love him. That is the way to know whether or not we live in him" (1 John 2:5).

Implications of Inspiration

Because the Scriptures come from God, every part is important, no matter how small. Jesus himself said, "I tell you the truth, until heaven and earth disappear, not the smallest letter, not the least stroke of a pen, will by any means disappear from the Law until everything is accomplished" (Matthew 5:18, NIV). The smallest Hebrew letter was *yod* (׳), which looks like an apostrophe. The "least stroke of a pen" refers to the small marks that differentiate one letter from another, such as *dalet* (ד) from *resh* (ר).

According to Jesus, the small extension from the top line of a dalet in the midst of the Law will last longer than the heavens and earth. Why? Because God breathed out the Law. Therefore it is as permanent as he is. Isaiah echoed the permanence of God's Word when he declared, "The grass withers, and the flowers fade beneath the breath of the LORD. And so it is with people. The grass withers, and the flowers fade, but the word of our God stands forever" (Isaiah 40:7-8). Peter quoted this passage from Isaiah in 1 Peter 1:23-25 with a twist. Peter asserted that the reason we know our new life in Christ will last forever is because it comes from the "eternal, living word of God." This living Word produces life within us, as well as reveals the innermost thoughts and secrets inside our souls (see Hebrews 4:12).

Not only will the words of the Bible last because they come from God; they also cannot be altered or nullified by people. In John 10:35, Jesus said that the Scriptures cannot be broken. In Revelation 22:18-19, John pronounced a divine curse on anyone who tries to add to or take away from the words of the final book of the Bible.

That wasn't the first time God placed such importance on his Word. Throughout the Bible he held people responsible for whether or not they obeyed his Word. He did this because, according to the Bible, the Scriptures truly are the very words of God. Because the Scriptures come from God, they carry his authority. Obeying God means obeying his word as found in the Bible. Deuteronomy 5:32 puts it this way: "You must obey all the commands of the LORD your God, following his instructions in every detail."

Skeptics pass off citing the Bible to show the truthfulness and authority of the Scriptures as circular reasoning. We will discuss this further in the section on inerrancy. However, for now suffice it to say that throughout the history of the church, Christians have generally agreed upon the divine nature, inspiration, and authority of the Bible. Without it, we would know nothing of Jesus Christ, who is the basis of Christianity in the first place.

QUESTIONS

Which Bible is the right Bible?

After hearing how vital the Bible is to the Christian life, many believers immediately ask, "Which one?" Since the beginning of the twentieth century, the number of English versions of the Bible has exploded. Does older mean better, or should all the old versions such as the King James and New International Versions be scrapped when a new Bible such as the New Living Translation or The Message comes along? The question isn't just one of taste or style. The real issue is this: Is one Bible version more authoritative than another? Is there only one *right* Bible?

Bible Basics

When speaking of different versions of the Bible, we don't refer to completely different Bibles with different books, characters, authors, and basic teachings.[11] Instead, we refer to different translations. The Old Testament was written in Hebrew and the New Testament in Greek. In Islam, Muslims — regardless of their backgrounds — have historically been required to learn Arabic to read the Koran in its original language. By contrast, Christians make translating the Bible into the native tongue of believers a priority as a part of fulfilling Jesus' command to make disciples of all nations. The Bible was first translated even before Jesus was born. Jewish scholars in Alexandria, Egypt, translated the Old Testament from Hebrew into Greek around 100 BC. Known as the Septuagint, this translation met the needs of a growing Jewish population who both spoke and read only Greek rather than Hebrew.

John Wycliffe compiled the first English translation of both the Old and New Testaments in 1380. William Tyndale translated the first modern English Bible — that is, the first

to be published after Johann Gutenberg invented the print-
ing press in 1436—in the sixteenth century. He published his
English New Testament in 1526 and the entire Bible in 1534.
In 1607, a team of scholars commissioned by King James I
started work on a new translation authorized by the throne.
Completed in 1611, the Authorized Version is better known as
the King James Version. It is estimated that nine-tenths of the
Authorized Version is taken from Tyndale's translation.[12] The
KJV was revised in 1613, 1629, and again in 1638. Finally, the
language and spelling were modernized at Cambridge in 1762
and at Oxford in 1769. These final revisions are essentially the
King James Bible we have today.[13]

The Authorized Version underwent revisions for the same
reason new translations continue to come on the scene.
Languages constantly change. As word meanings and phrases
evolve and change, translations must be updated. If not, they
soon cease to fulfill the purpose of translating the Bible, which
is to allow modern readers to read the ancient texts without
first spending a lifetime learning Hebrew and Greek. C. S.
Lewis said, "The truth is that if we are to have translation at all
we must have periodical re-translation. There is no such thing
as translating a book into a language once for all, for a language
is a changing thing. If your son is to have clothes it is no good
buying him a suit once and for all: he will grow out of it and
have to be re-clothed."[14]

Principles of Translation

Scholars use two approaches when translating the Bible
as they attempt to balance faithfulness to the original text
with readability in the translation. The first approach,
formal equivalence, works to render a word-for-word, literal

translation. The second, dynamic equivalence, focuses on giving a thought-for-thought rendering of the text. The New American Standard, King James Version, and New King James are the most literal of the popular translations, while the New Living Translation is the best example of dynamic equivalence. The New International Version attempts to strike a balance between formal and dynamic equivalence.

The Message and The Living Bible are not translations in the classic sense, but paraphrases of the Bible — that is, they restate the message of the Scriptures in modern vernacular. While other translations employ a team of scholars, paraphrases are primarily the work of one person, although a team of scholars oversees the projects.

So which approach is best, formal or dynamic equivalence? The question comes down to readability versus accuracy. All translations, even the most literal, must at times translate thought for thought. For example, Acts 20:7 contains the phrase, "τῇ μιᾷ τῶν σαββάτων," which literally reads, "the one of the Sabbaths." However, in this context, the word "Sabbaths" means "week." The "one" means the first day, or, the first day of the week. A strict reliance on literal accuracy would leave the translation unintelligible.

In the same way, emphasizing readability can, at times, give a technically accurate translation while losing some of the details within the text. For example, in Romans 3:25, Paul calls Jesus the ἱλαστήριον that God gave for our sins. The Greek term literally means "mercy seat," which connects Jesus to the Old Testament Day of Atonement and the place where the blood of the sacrifice was sprinkled within the Holy of Holies. That doesn't mean "mercy seat" is the best way to translate the term. No major translation uses this choice of words. While a literal translation of the term does not convey the full weight of Paul's message, losing the word-for-word translation causes English-speaking readers to miss the parallels Paul wanted to convey.

Translations and Interpretation

Every translation carries an element of commentary on the text. The English words translators choose reflect a degree of their own theological outlook, no matter how hard they may try to do otherwise. Romans 3:25 above is the best example of this. The Greek term ἱλαστήριον conveys the idea of making atonement and forgiving sin. However, a question remains as to whether the emphasis needs to be placed on the one who has been sinned against, or the act that needs to be forgiven. The former places the emphasis on God, who is angry because of our sin and whose wrath must be satisfied. The latter puts the emphasis on humans and the things we've done that broke God's Law.

In the first half of the twentieth century, the debate came down to which of two words should be used to translate this term, propitiation or expiation. Propitiation means to regain the good will or mercy of an offended party, while expiation means to extinguish the guilt incurred by sin. The King James Version, along with the American Standard Version of 1901 and the New American Standard Bible, used propitiation. The Revised Standard Version (1946, 1952) sparked a great deal of controversy when it used expiation instead.

Twenty-first-century readers fail to grasp the reason for the debate, because neither term means anything to the major-ity of believers, especially those under forty. However, the way modern translations render the term still reveals the translators' understanding of which idea should be the focal point of the verse: God's anger or human guilt. The New Living Translation emphasizes the former by translating Romans 3:25 as, "For God sent Jesus to take the punishment for our sins and to satisfy God's anger against us." The NIV focuses on the latter: "God presented him as a sacrifice of atonement," although a footnote reads, "Or *as the one who would turn aside his wrath, taking away sin.*"

The point is simply this: Every translation reflects the biases of the translators, no matter how subtle those biases may be. That's why the major translations use a large number of scholars from across the theological spectrum to make the resulting version as nonsectarian as possible.

The Best Translation

All of this brings us back to the question posed at the beginning: Which translation is the best translation? The answer isn't easy to give. Every translation has both strengths and weaknesses. Therefore, short of spending the next twenty years of your life working to become proficient at both Greek and Hebrew, the best approach is to read and compare multiple translations. By comparing different versions, we are able to pick up on the different shades of meaning and nuances of the original language. Changing translations from time to time also keeps God's Word fresh. We can become so accustomed to the sound and rhythm of our favorite translation that we fail to hear God speak through it. Using a different translation can wake us up and allow us to hear the Bible again.

Does this mean all translations are equally good? Not at all. But, by comparing translations, you can discern the intent of the original authors of the Bible. When one version uses radically different words that give a completely different meaning from all the rest, a red flag should come up telling you something is awry.

Can the Bible ever be wrong?

Christians believe the Bible is God's Word. However, parts of the Bible are very difficult to understand and believe, especially in light of modern scientific advances. The first chapter of the Bible says God created plants before he created the sun, moon, and stars. How is that possible? Other passages appear to contradict one another. Second Samuel 24:1 says God was angry with Israel and incited King David to sin by taking a census. However, 1 Chronicles 21:1 says Satan was responsible for doing this. Second Samuel 24:1 also appears to contradict James 1:13, which says God never tempts anyone to do evil. Does this mean the writer of 2 Samuel was mistaken? Or is James wrong? Or is it possible that both are correct?

The Bible also contains data that doesn't add up using basic scientific methods. For example, 2 Chronicles 4:1-2 describes a large round tank called "the Sea" that sat near the entrance of the temple. The priests washed in this tank before performing their sacred duties. The writer of Chronicles said the Sea was ten cubits wide and thirty cubits in circumference. However, you learned in math class that you find the circumference of a circle by multiplying π by the diameter, which would make the Sea 31.4 cubits around rather than 30. Does this mean the Bible made a mistake and is therefore in error?

The real question is this: Can the Bible ever be wrong?

Inerrancy and Infallibility

The question of whether or not the Bible contains mistakes or wrong information is called the question of *inerrancy*. Historically, evangelical Christians have maintained that the Bible is free of error and is therefore completely trustworthy.

The statement of faith for The Navigators, the parent company of TH1NK, states the doctrine like this: "We believe that the Scriptures of the Old and New Testaments are inspired by God and inerrant in the original writings, and that they are of supreme and final authority in faith and life."

Closely related to the idea of inerrancy is that of infallibility. This means that the Bible never makes false or misleading statements. Infallibility means God's Word is always correct when it speaks. Both inerrancy and infallibility grow out of the doctrine of the Bible's divine nature and inspiration. If the Bible is God's Word, the logical conclusion is that he will always tell us the truth, and his Word will be error free.

Inerrancy applies only to the original writings. Only the Scriptures as originally written by Moses, Paul, and the other authors of the Bible are free of error. Subsequent copies and translations share this to the degree that they match the originals. Critics claim this dances around the issue, because the originals no longer exist. However, through textual criticism — that is, comparing the large number of ancient copies of the Bible with one another — scholars are able to tell with a fair degree of certainty where a copyist error may have crept into the biblical text.

Stating the doctrine in this way also protects against a blanket endorsement of all translations, because errors can creep into the publication process. A 1631 edition of the Authorized Version was known as the "Wicked Bible" because a typesetter forgot to put a "not" in the seventh commandment. Imagine the surprise that greeted everyone who read, "Thou shalt commit adultery."

Most formal declarations on biblical inerrancy also include the phrase "when translated correctly." Millard Erickson built his definition of the term around this idea by stating, "The Bible, *when correctly interpreted* in light of the level to which culture and the means of communication had developed at the time it was written, and in view of the purposes for which it was given, is fully truthful in all that it affirms."[15] Why this caveat? While the Bible may be true in all it affirms, the conclusions believers draw from it may not be correct, even when those conclusions enjoy universal popularity. For example, prior to the Copernican revolution in science, people thought the Bible taught that the earth was the center of the universe. The Bible wasn't in error; what people read into it was.

Views of Inerrancy

Those who believe the Bible is error free differ on the scope of inerrancy. *Absolute inerrantists* maintain that the Bible is completely true in everything it says, even when it gives historical and scientific details. They believe the Bible's writers intended to give us not only information about God and how to know him, but also detailed scientific and historical information.

Full inerrantists also hold that the Bible is completely true, even in matters of science and history. However, they would say that the Bible records scientific and historical information as they appear to the observer, rather than as a scientist or a historian would write about them.

Limited inerrantists also believe the Bible is free from error, but only in reference to matters directly related to faith and salvation, not science and history.

Finally, there are those who say that the Bible is *inerrant in purpose,* and that purpose is to bring people into a relationship with Christ, not to communicate truth.[16]

The best way to understand the difference is to see each view in action. Absolute inerrantists read the first chapter of Genesis and say that God spoke the heavens and the earth into existence in six literal twenty-four-hour days. Full inerrantists say God created the universe in six days; however, the "days" don't necessarily mean twenty-four-hour periods, but rather six distinct ages of creative activity by God. These ages could have been as short as a day or as long as thousands upon thousands of years. Limited inerrantists believe the question of the length of the days or how God created everything is irrelevant. The important truth is the fact that God made everything, whether that was in six days, in six ages, or over an incredibly long period of time through evolutionary processes. The last group, those who hold to inerrancy of purpose, would say that the important truth of Genesis 1 is simply that there is a God who speaks and can be known. To them, the Bible was never meant to communicate objective truths about the origins of the universe.

Inerrancy and Questionable Passages

The question of inerrancy stops being just another theological debate the moment you open your Bible and read something that is hard to believe or appears to contradict itself. At that moment you have to ask yourself, *Can I trust what I am reading?* For example, what do you do with a passage like Joshua 10:13, which says, "So the sun and moon stood still until the Israelites had defeated their enemies. Is this event not recorded in *The Book of Jashar*? The sun stopped in the middle of the sky, and it did not set as on a normal day"?

For the limited inerrantist or those who limit inerrancy to the Bible's overall purpose, this passage doesn't pose a problem.

They would say the sun didn't stand still, since the earth would have to stop spinning on its axis to make this happen. To them, Joshua records a myth or legend that was meant to convey a lesson on faith.

Those holding a stronger view of inerrancy approach difficult passages with the understanding that just because a passage is hard to understand doesn't mean it's false or figurative. From beginning to end, the Bible records miraculous events, all of which defy what we consider normal. In fact, the central truth upon which Christianity rests is hard to understand on a strictly human level. How could God become flesh, be born of a virgin, live a sinless life, die on a cross, and rise bodily from the dead? Yet 1 Corinthians 15:17-19 declares that if these events did not take place, Christianity is a sham. Paul wrote, "If Christ has not been raised, then your faith is useless, and you are still under condemnation for your sins. In that case, all who have died believing in Christ have perished! And if we have hope in Christ only for this life, we are the most miserable people in the world."

How then would they deal with a verse like Joshua 10:13? Most would admit that they don't know how God kept the sun from setting, but they believe that he did it just as the Bible says. Full inerrantists would also add that the sun stood still from the perspective of the observer on the battlefield, so the earth did not have to stop spinning to make this miracle happen.

Apparent discrepancies in the Bible are handled in the same way. For example, the relation of the circumference to the diameter of the large tank at the entrance to the temple mentioned at the beginning of this chapter isn't an example of the Bible being wrong. Instead, the author of Chronicles describes this as an observer. He isn't giving technical data. Those holding to a strong view of inerrancy believe that explanations exist for these difficult passages, even if they do not yet know what they may be.

Does the Question Matter?

During the 1970s and 1980s, inerrancy was *the* hot-button issue among evangelicals. Harold Lindsell in his book *The Battle for the Bible* called it the single most important question facing Christianity. He and other leaders of the day saw inerrancy as the dividing line between true believers and those who had stepped onto the slippery slope toward unbelief. While he stopped short of saying that those who did not believe in inerrancy were not truly Christians, the implication was that those who did not hold this view were in danger of abandoning the faith. The Chicago Statement on Biblical Inerrancy declared, "We affirm that a confession of the full authority, infallibility, and inerrancy of Scripture is vital to a sound understanding of the whole of the Christian faith."

Both the Southern Baptist Convention (the largest Protestant denomination in America) and the Lutheran Church–Missouri Synod went through protracted internal battles over inerrancy. In both cases, those holding to a strict view of inerrancy carried the day. Both denominations marked the outcomes of these disputes as major victories for the integrity of God's Word and the Lord's work on earth.

Today, however, leaders of the Emerging Church movement and other younger evangelicals shy away from using the term. They do so for two reasons. First, to them the word *inerrancy* is a negative term, describing something the Bible is not, rather than something it is. Further, they point out that the Bible never uses the term to describe itself. When asked their view of the Word of God, they prefer to use vocabulary the biblical writers used—terms such as "living, active, profitable for teaching, and truth."[17]

The second reason lies in the roots of the debate over inerrancy and the emergence of the term in the evangelical theological vocabulary. Much of the writings on and in defense of inerrancy grew out of response to the Enlightenment questions on epistemology—that is, the question of how we can know what we know. Enlightenment thinkers sought to find the base or foundation for all knowledge, which is known as foundationalism. Prior to this time, the church and the Bible were viewed as the starting point for all knowledge, at least in the Western world during the Middle Ages. Enlightenment thought pushed God and the Bible to the side and sought a universal ground for knowledge that did not depend on special revelation.[18]

Theologians responded by seeking a ground of sure knowledge for Christianity. Two schools of thought emerged, liberals and conservatives. Generally speaking, liberals looked for this foundation apart from the Bible and pointed to religious experience as the answer. Conservatives said the Bible, the Word of God, is the one sure foundation for all knowledge, and within this Word are authoritative, propositional truths that can be clearly stated in a timeless way.[19]

The problem with both approaches, according to Stanley Grenz and John Franke, is that in their quest to find the foundational truth upon which all knowledge can be based, both liberal and conservative theologians silenced the Bible. The Scriptures themselves and the stories that fill them ceased to be primary. Instead, these theologians read the Bible only to discover the timeless, propositional truths beneath the text. As a result, the story of David and Goliath mattered far less than the lessons it teaches about God's ability to defeat any foe. Instead of someone reading the Bible for himself, a person needed an expert to come along and tell him what the text is really about. And believing the experts' explanation of these timeless truths became equated with believing the inerrant Bible. As Grenz and Franke put it, "Despite the well-meaning, lofty intentions of conservative thinkers to honor the Bible as Scripture, their approach in effect contributed to the silencing of the text in the church."[20]

The Emerging Church removes itself from the entire debate over inerrancy and its foundationalist roots by asserting that Christianity doesn't need a rational defense. In his book *The Younger Evangelicals,* Robert Webber states, "Radical Orthodoxy begins with the assumption that Christianity is truth. Because it is true, everything in the world—the world itself, its history, its religions, its social sciences, its ethics, its behaviors—should be interpreted and understood through the Christian faith."[21] They feel no need to prove the Bible is free of errors. Postmodern theologians simply begin with the Bible and let it determine what is real. Rather than search for a way to explain away the hard-to-understand and mysterious, this school of thought declares we should simply let God's story speak. As God speaks, lives will be changed.

Does this approach dodge the question that started this chapter? That's for you to decide.

2

God

ESSENTIALS

Who is like the Lord?

The Trinity: One God, Three Persons

QUESTIONS

When did God make everything?

How can God be good with so much bad in the world?

How can God be in control and people still be free?

When God told Moses to go to the people of Israel and tell them the God of their fathers had heard their cries for help, Moses asked a simple question that people continue to ask today: Which god are you talking about? Polls consistently show that around 90 percent of Americans believe in God, but that doesn't necessarily mean they all believe in the God of the Bible. Yet even among those who claim to believe in the same God, beliefs vary widely. God's name is bandied about by everyone from athletes after making a great play to entertainers accepting awards to protesters trying to get their way in Washington. Listening to all the rhetoric, we have to ask, which god are you talking about?

Christianity finds the answer in the pages of the Bible. God is not whoever or whatever we want to make him out to be. Instead, God himself reveals his true character to us through his Word. The true identity of God isn't up in the air for each of us to decide on our own. He tells us who he is, and he does so for a reason.

Through the centuries theologians have used many words to describe God, most of which are long, hard to pronounce, and meaningless to the uninitiated—words such as omniscient, omnipotent, and transcendent. As a result, reading theology leaves many people reaching for a pillow as their eyelids grow heavier and heavier.

That is a tragedy. Contemplating God and his wonder should leave us in awe and cause us to open our mouths to sing his praises. The psalmist declared:

> Great is the LORD! He is most worthy of praise!
>   His greatness is beyond discovery!
> Let each generation tell its children
>   of your mighty acts.
> I will meditate on your majestic, glorious splendor
>   and your wonderful miracles.
> Your awe-inspiring deeds will be on every tongue;
>   I will proclaim your greatness.
> Everyone will share the story of your wonderful
>   goodness;
>   they will sing with joy of your righteousness.
>   (Psalm 145:3-7)

As we explore who God is and what he does, this is our goal as well.

John Calvin said we should adore God rather than try to pry into his essence with presumptive curiosity.[1] Yet pry we must, for so many ideas float around our culture as to who God is and what he does. However, as we do, let us heed the words of Jonathan Edwards: "It is easily proved that the highest end and happiness of man is to *view God's excellency,* to *love* him, and *receive expressions* of his love."[2]

ESSENTIALS

Who is like the Lord?

"Who else among the gods is like you, O Lord? Who is glorious in holiness like you—so awesome in splendor, performing such wonders?" Moses declared in a song he composed after God parted the Red Sea (Exodus 15:11). Don't let the question marks fool you. These questions are purely rhetorical because the answer is a resounding, "NO ONE!" There is no other god like the Lord, because he alone is God. All the rest are nothing but human inventions and poor imitations. "I am the First and the Last; there is no other God," the Lord declares in Isaiah 44:6.

The quest to understand God begins here. The God of the Bible declares that he alone is God. Moreover, he declares that there is only one Way by which he can be known. Jesus said, "I am the way, the truth, and the life. No one can come to the Father except through me" (John 14:6). What this means is simply this: When we talk about the God of the Bible, we are not talking about the same god worshiped by Muslims, nor are we talking about the gods of Hinduism or the god or gods of any other world religion. The God of the Bible stands apart not only as unique, but also as the only genuine article.[3] Believing in *a* god is not the point. All the belief in the world doesn't mean a thing if it isn't aimed in the right direction.

Who then is this God, and what is he like?

Eternal

Everything in the universe has a beginning and will eventually end—everything except God. Those rules don't apply to him, because he made them. Before there was time, God was there. And when time comes to an end, he still will be. He has always been and he will always be, for God is eternal. As the psalmist sang, "Before the mountains were created, before you made the earth and the world, you are God, without beginning or end" (Psalm 90:2).

No outside force made God. Life begins with him. He exists completely independent of everything else that exists, with a life that never runs down or wears out. The Author of life lives a life that does not have a finite starting point and will never end. God's eternal nature means more than he lives forever. It tells us that his essential being never changes. He doesn't need periodic makeovers or tune-ups, because physical laws of entropy don't apply to him. The quality of his life remains the same for all of eternity.

God's eternal nature also means he never changes. "I am the Lord, and I do not change," God says in Malachi 3:6. He remains consistent. He will not require one thing of you today and something else completely tomorrow. That's why we can count on the promises God made in the Bible, even though he gave them around two thousand years ago. Because God doesn't change, neither does his Word. We can cling to it just as believers have since the day God directed Moses to pen the first words of the Bible.

Creator Extraordinaire

"In the beginning God created the heavens and the earth," the Bible starts off in Genesis 1. We can reduce this to a simple statement: God made everything. While technically correct, so much more needs to be said. God didn't just make everything; he made everything beautiful and wonderful and awe-inspiring. When he created the heavens and the earth, he didn't just get out his toolbox. He pulled out his artist's palette and started having fun. He splashed color from one end of the universe to the other, and then he designed subtle ways to keep the show constantly moving before our eyes. From the glory of a sunset to the startling beauty of a frosty Indiana morning, God's artistry never gets old. Words cannot describe it, although that doesn't keep us from trying. About the time we get used to the wonder of nature around us, God pulls our eyes toward the sky with a telescope or downward through a microscope to marvel over the intricate detail of his design. Yes, he is the Creator of all things. But he is more than that. The God of the Bible is the ultimate Artist whose masterpiece can never be matched.

Powerful

God has the power to do anything and everything he desires. Nothing is too difficult for him. The Bible declares, "The LORD merely spoke, and the heavens were created. He breathed the word, and all the stars were born" (Psalm 33:6). But that's only the beginning. Throughout the Bible we see God's power unleashed. In Genesis he flooded the entire earth but saved Noah and his family. In Exodus, God humbled the mightiest nation through plagues. Then he set the Israelites free once and for all by parting the Red Sea. In Joshua and Judges, his power gave Israel the Promised Land, and in 1 Samuel, it enabled David to defeat Goliath. It protected Shadrach, Meshach, and Abednego in the fiery furnace in the book of Daniel and kept the lions from harming Daniel when he was thrown into a pit full of them. Ultimately, God's power raised Jesus from the dead and thereby conquered death once and for all.

Believing that God is powerful is easy. Faith comes in when we not only believe that God is able to create galaxies and nebulae and black holes in the far corners of space, but also that he has the power to make good on his promises even when it looks like he has forgotten us. Romans 4 tells us this was the kind of faith Abraham exercised when he believed God would give him and his wife a son, even though they were both pushing one hundred years of age. This is what it means to believe God is all-powerful. When our lives take turns we never wanted them to take, when everything around us screams that God can't help us no matter how hard we pray, in those moments, we must decide how powerful we believe God really is. Is he strong enough to do what he promised?

Passionate

First John 4:8 simply says, "God is love." The most recognizable verse in the Bible says, "For God so loved the world that he gave his only Son" (John 3:16). Of all the qualities of God that we innately understand, this is the strongest. All people everywhere may not understand God's love, but they all crave a God who will love them. Love starts with God. John also wrote, "We love because he first loved us" (1 John 4:19, NIV).

Although we know that God loves us, we often fail to grasp the depths of his love. He doesn't just have a strong affection that he shows from time to time at a distance, like a faraway grandfather who pats you on the head and hands you a twenty-dollar bill when you see him once or twice a year. The Bible paints pictures of God's love that show a breathtaking passion. He loves us like a proud father and like a mother gazing at her newborn child for the first time. But his love doesn't stop there. The Bible says God loves us like a bridegroom gazing into the eyes of his bride on their wedding day. That's what makes human sin so painful to God.

One of the best pictures of God's passion is found in Ezekiel 16. Set this book aside and go read it right now. If possible, read it in The Message.[4] Eugene Peterson does a fantastic job of capturing the intense emotions God feels both as he chooses to love us and as he watches the object of his love turn her back on him. Ezekiel's word picture will help you understand what the Bible means when it says, "God is love."

Wise

God knows what he's doing. He doesn't need someone to explain the complexities of the postmodern world to him, nor does he struggle to figure out a way to fix all the messes the human race creates for itself. His wisdom so outstrips human wisdom that people think him foolish (see 1 Corinthians 1:18-23). Because he composed the deepest mysteries of the universe, he doesn't need someone to tell him what to do. Romans 11:33-35 declares:

> Have you ever come on anything quite like this extravagant generosity of God, this deep, deep wisdom? It's way over our heads. We'll never figure it out.
>
> Is there anyone around who can explain God?
> Anyone smart enough to tell him what to do?
> Anyone who has done him such a huge favor
>   that God has to ask his advice? (MSG)

That is what we mean when we say God is wise. He knows what he's doing, even when we don't understand what he's up to.

Merciful

The book of Jonah presents one of the sharpest contrasts between human beings and God. There we find that the difference between him and us goes far deeper than his eternal qualities, his wisdom and power. The real difference between almighty God and finite human beings lies within our hearts. God delights in granting people forgiveness, especially those who seem least worthy of it. Human history shows that people enjoy holding grudges. Go read the book of Jonah, and then you'll understand what God's mercy is all about.

God is merciful to a degree that humans rarely approach. Yes, God punishes sin, but only as a last resort. "Do you think I take any pleasure in the death of wicked men and women?" God asked through Ezekiel. "Isn't it my pleasure that they turn around, no longer living wrong but living right—really living?" (Ezekiel 18:23, MSG). When people do turn to him, he pours out his love on them. In Deuteronomy 5:10, he promises to "lavish my love on those who love me and obey my commands, even for a thousand generations." A generation is the average interval between the births of parents and the births of their children. Ask your parents how old they were when you were born and do the math. That's how long God plans on showing his mercy and grace toward the descendants of those who turn to him.

Faithful

God always keeps his promises. The book of Numbers tells us, "God is not a man, that he should lie. He is not a human, that he should change his mind. Has he ever spoken and failed to act? Has he ever promised and not carried it through?" (23:19). The answer is, of course, no. He always follows through on what he vows to do.

God's faithfulness does even more. He remains loyal to those he has pledged to love, regardless of what they may do. Paul put it this way: "If we are unfaithful, he remains faithful, for he cannot deny himself" (2 Timothy 2:13). To fully appreciate this truth, you need to see it in action. Read the book of Judges. Pay close attention to everything the Israelites put God through, yet he never abandons them. He remains faithful to them even though they don't reciprocate. God never changes, nor does his faithfulness both to his Word and to his children.

Holy

The angels in heaven are singing a song right now as you read these words on this page. They continually cry out, "Holy, holy, holy is the Lord God Almighty—the one who always was, who is, and who is still to come" (Revelation 4:8). Isaiah recorded the same song in heaven's temple in Isaiah 6. When the Bible wants to emphasize something, it repeats. Those things of utmost importance it repeats three times. That is why the angels sing, "Holy, holy, holy." Above all else, our God is holy.

The word *holy* means set apart, sacred. When used to describe God, it refers to his absolute purity and righteousness. We may say of people, "Well, nobody's perfect," but we can't say that of God. Everything he does is right and true and altogether holy. He cannot be tempted by evil, and he will never tempt anyone to do anything wrong (see James 1:13).

God's holiness also means nothing sinful can come near him any more than darkness can approach a blazing 2 million-candlepower spotlight. This is what creates the divine dilemma when it comes to human beings. God loves us with an undying passion, yet every member of the human race has sinned and falls short of his glory (see Romans 3:23). How then can a holy

God find a way not only to forgive sin, but also to remove its offense and thus open the door for people to know him personally? We will discuss the answer in the section on Jesus.

Frightening

Most of us rarely associate the word *frightening* with God, yet this is the picture we see of him in the Bible. Adam and Eve hid in the garden as fear gripped them when they heard the sound of God approaching. The sound of his voice at Mount Sinai caused the Israelites to cry out in terror, asking God to leave them alone and speak only to Moses. Even those closest to the Lord trembled in his presence. Isaiah caught a glimpse of God in his holiness and fell on his face, begging for mercy. We see this same sort of fear with the disciples in the boat when Jesus calmed the sea.

Of course, what else should we expect? If a loud rattling sound coming from behind a rock in the dry, rattlesnake-infested hills of western Oklahoma makes the hair on the backs of our necks stand up, how much more so should the prospect of coming face-to-face with the One who holds the universe in his hand? The Bible says the fear of the Lord is wisdom (see Job 28:28). This fear means more than respect and more than awe. A glimpse into the true nature of the living God should scare the socks off of us.

Near

Moses asked the Israelites, "What other nation is so great as to have their gods near them the way the LORD our God is near us whenever we pray to him?" (Deuteronomy 4:7, NIV). His nearness to his children sets our God apart from all the pretenders. After creating the universe, he didn't retire to a corner of heaven, only to peer down on earth when he grew bored with the angels' singing. Over and over in the Bible we see how God stays close by those who love him. Psalm 46:1 declares, "God is our refuge and strength, always ready to help in times of trouble."

When we say God is near, this is what we mean. His presence surrounds those who fear him, and he comes to our aid when we need him most (see Psalm 34:7).

King

"The LORD is king! Let the nations tremble! He sits on his throne between the cherubim. Let the whole earth quake!" Psalm 99:1 announces. Empires and kingdoms may come and go. Dictators assert their power, and presidents declare themselves to be the leaders of the free world, yet ultimately, God and God alone rules the earth. He is the King of kings and the Lord of lords. Every earthly power will ultimately bow before his throne. Unlike human kings, the Lord reigns with justice. He fights for the oppressed and holds accountable those who abuse earthly power.

This truth is easy to declare, yet often hard to see in the real world. Living in a world filled with violence and suffering makes us wonder how much control the Lord exercises. That's when we must balance the fact that God rules the universe with the fact that he has given human beings free will. While believers differ on where to strike this balance (which we discuss in a later chapter in this section), they all agree that ultimately, the Lord is King over all. One day he will establish his kingdom in a more visible way, eliminating the effects of sin once and for all.

Good

The first prayer many of us learned to pray focused on God's goodness: "God is great, God is good. . . ." His goodness pervades everything God does. It spills over in his acts of love and mercy. He will always do not only what is right, but also what is best for those he loves.

It would be easy to digress here to a mushy-gushy discussion that ends with us all sitting around a campfire singing "Kumbayah." (Not that that's a bad thing.) Yet we shouldn't mistake God's goodness with a syrupy softness that allows us to run over him. Nor should we assume that a good God wants no more than to make our lives trouble free. Again, God's love drives him to do what will accomplish the greatest eternal good in the lives of those he loves. Like Aslan, the lion in C. S. Lewis's *The Lion, the Witch and the Wardrobe*, our God may be good, but that doesn't make him safe.

The Trinity: One God, Three Persons

When Christians ask, "Who is God?" the answer invariably leads to one place: the Trinity. We believe in one God who reveals himself as a tri-unity of three distinct persons: Father, Son, and Holy Spirit. Although the word doesn't appear in the Bible, it has separated true Christianity from perversions of the truth since the days of the ancient church. The reason is simple: If you err on who God is, the rest of your theology is irrelevant. It's like missing the first step in a ten-part algebra equation. No matter how well you do on the final nine steps, when step one arrives at the wrong sum, the final answer will never be correct.

As important as it is, most believers pass over the doctrine of the Trinity as boring stuff only theologians fully grasp. After all, wrapping your brain around the idea that three can be one without surrendering their distinctiveness and while also main-taining their essential oneness gives most people a headache. Rather than try to understand it, most prefer to simply say they believe it and move on.

Yet the triune nature of God touches every part of the Christian life, both for individuals and for communities of faith. Believers stretching back to the beginning of time first experienced God as he revealed himself to Israel, then through the Person and work of Jesus Christ, and finally through the indwelling presence of the Holy Spirit. When we open the Bible, we discover there is only one God, yet the Father and the Son and the Holy Spirit are all referred to as God, although they are clearly distinguished from one another.

Even the act of salvation is a triune act of God. We seek the Father, but the only way we can reach him is to go through the One who bridges the gap between God and human beings,

Jesus Christ. Then, once we reach the Father, we realize that the desire that made us seek him in the first place didn't come from us but from the Spirit working in us. All three members of the Trinity actively worked to bring us into God's family. We may not understand the Trinity, but if we're Christians, we've experienced him already.

The working of the triune God in our lives doesn't stop the moment we turn to Jesus Christ as our Savior. The simple act of prayer immerses us in the daily work of the Trinity. In his classic work *Mere Christianity*, C. S. Lewis put it this way:

> An ordinary simple Christian kneels down to say his prayers. He is trying to get into touch with God. But if he is a Christian he knows that what is prompting him to pray is also God: God, so to speak, inside him. But he also knows that all his real knowledge of God comes through Christ, the Man who was God—that Christ is standing beside him, helping him to pray, praying for him. You see what is happening. God is the thing to which he is praying—the goal he is trying to reach. God is also the thing inside him which is pushing him on—the motive power. God is also the road or bridge along which he is being pushed to that goal. So that the whole threefold life of the three-personal Being is actually going on in that ordinary little bedroom where an ordinary man is saying his prayers.[5]

One yet Three in the Bible

The word *Trinity* may not appear in the Bible, but the truth of this doctrine permeates the entire book. "I am the LORD your God, who rescued you from slavery in Egypt. Do not worship any other gods besides me," the Ten Commandments begin (Exodus 20:2-3). The message is simple: The Lord alone is God, and there are no others. From beginning to end, this is the message of the Old Testament. Deuteronomy 6:4 (NIV) declares, "Hear, O Israel: The LORD our God, the LORD is one."

The New Testament echoes this refrain as it builds on what came before it. James rebuked those who thought that believing facts about God without doing anything about them was enough when he wrote, "Do you still think it's enough just to believe that there is one God? Well, even the demons believe this, and they tremble in terror!" (James 2:19). Paul also declared the oneness of God when he told the Corinthians, "But we know that there is only one God, the Father, who created everything, and we exist for him. And there is only one Lord, Jesus Christ, through whom God made everything and through whom we have been given life" (1 Corinthians 8:6). Jesus declared the oneness of God when he told the Pharisees that the first and greatest command- ment is to "love the Lord your God with all your heart, all your soul, and all your mind" (Matthew 22:37).

Yet the Bible also refers to Jesus as God. The faith confession of ancient Israel was, "The Lord is God," yet the faith confession of New Testament believers (who also firmly believed the Lord is God) was, "Jesus is Lord." The Greek word that refers to God as the Lord in the Septuagint is the same word used of Jesus throughout the New Testament: the word κυριος. Other passages make it clear what this means. Hebrews 1:3 says, "The Son reflects God's own glory, and everything about him repre- sents God exactly. He sustains the universe by the mighty power of his command." Paul wrote of Jesus in Philippians 2:6-7, "Though he was God, he did not demand and cling to his rights as God. He made himself nothing; he took the humble position of a slave and appeared in human form."

Jesus acknowledged his own deity throughout his life. He spoke of the angels of God as his angels (see Matthew 13:41) and equated the kingdom of God with his own kingdom (see Matthew 12:28; 19:14,24). He also claimed the authority to forgive sins. The Pharisees howled in protest at this claim, saying only God had the authority to do such a thing (see Mark 2:1-11). Jesus also allowed people to worship him, even accepting Thomas's declaration of praise, "My Lord and my God!" (John 20:28).

The Bible also refers to the Holy Spirit of God. He was there when God created everything, moving over the surface of the deep (see Genesis 1:2). Throughout the Old Testament he is called the Spirit of God, and he enables God's people to do extraordinary things. In the New Testament, he is specifically equated with God. The best example is found in Acts 5. A man named Ananias and his wife Sapphira hatched a scheme to sell a plot of ground, keep part of the money for themselves, and give the rest to the apostles, while claiming that they were giving it all to them. Why would they do such a thing? They wanted people to praise them for their generosity, but they also wanted some money from their land. Peter rebuked them: "Ananias, why has Satan filled your heart? You lied to the Holy Spirit, and you kept some of the money for yourself. The property was yours to sell or not sell, as you wished. And after selling it, the money was yours to give away. How could you do a thing like this? You weren't lying to us but to God" (Acts 5:3-4). Peter equated the Holy Spirit with God. Elsewhere, the New Testament attributes deeds and character qualities of the Spirit as works of God.

The references to the deity of Jesus and the Spirit do not contradict the truth that God is one. Nor does the New

Testament teach that there are three gods. Instead, the three are linked together as one. At Jesus' birth, we find that the Father sent the Son, who was conceived through the Spirit. One of the best examples of the unity and equality of the three is found in Jesus' final words, also known as the Great Commission. There he told his disciples, "Therefore, go and make disciples of all the nations, baptizing them in the name of the Father and the Son and the Holy Spirit" (Matthew 28:19). Jesus made it clear that these three—Father, Son, and Spirit—are one when he told his followers to baptize in the name of all three. Paul placed the three on equal footing when he closed his second letter to the church in Corinth with the words, "May the grace of our Lord Jesus Christ, the love of God, and the fellowship of the Holy Spirit be with you all" (2 Corinthians 13:13).

Other examples of the tri-unity of the Father, Son, and Holy Spirit abound in the New Testament, especially in the gospel of John. John 1:1 declares, "In the beginning was the Word, and the Word was with God, and the Word was God" (NIV). A few verses later, the gospel writer showed that the Word refers to Jesus. Jesus claimed, "I and the Father are one" (John 10:30, NIV) and said that anyone who has seen him has seen the Father (see John 14:9). He said the Father would send the Spirit in the Son's name (see John 14:26), and when the Spirit came, he would glorify the Son (see John 16:13-14). Elsewhere, the Holy Spirit is called the Spirit of God (see Genesis 1:2; Matthew 3:16), as well as the Spirit of Christ (see Romans 8:9).

Explaining the Unexplainable

If the Trinity is so clearly revealed in the Bible and so vital to the Christian life, why is it so hard to understand? The answer takes us back to the question that runs through this entire section. The

Trinity is difficult to grasp because it describes God's essential nature. In wrestling with such a concept, we come face-to-face with the fact that God is not only much bigger and mightier than we are, but he is also completely different from us. C. S. Lewis compared our struggle to comprehend God's nature with a creature confined to two dimensions trying to comprehend the three-dimensional world. A mind programmed to think in terms of flat lines cannot find the right words to describe any shape that rises above it.[6]

This same problem strikes when we try to explain the triune nature of God or to find some analogy to which we can compare it. At best the analogies fall short; at worst they throw us into the realm of heresy. One such heresy is called *modalism*. This view teaches that there is only one God who appears to us in different ways at different times. At times the Father appears as the Son, and at other times he appears as the Spirit. In modalism, the three are not distinct from one another. Rather, they are simply roles God plays at different times. Although unintended, modalism lies beneath a popular analogy of the Trinity many preachers use when they compare God to themselves by saying, "I am a father, but I am also a son, and I possess a spirit." The same fallacy occurs when the Trinity is compared to the three forms of water: solid, liquid, and gas.

In its attempts to put this doctrine into words, the ancient church did not turn to analogies, but to written creeds. One of the earliest, the Nicene Creed, came about in response to a heresy called *Arianism*, which said Jesus was a created being rather than eternally God. In AD 325, the Council of Nicaea formulated the creed that was later expanded at the Council of Constantinople in 381. It states:

We believe in one God,
    the Father, the Almighty,
    maker of heaven and earth,
    of all that is, seen and unseen.
We believe in one Lord, Jesus Christ,
    the only Son of God,
    eternally begotten of the Father,
    God from God, Light from Light,
    true God from true God,
    begotten, not made,
    of one Being with the Father.
    Through Him all things were made.
For us and for our salvation
    He came down from heaven:
by the power of the Holy Spirit
    He became incarnate from the Virgin Mary,
    and was made man.
For our sake He was crucified under Pontius Pilate;
He suffered death and was buried.
On the third day He rose again
    in accordance with the Scriptures;
He ascended into heaven
    and is seated at the right hand of the Father.
He will come again in glory to judge the living and
    the dead,
    and His kingdom will have no end.
We believe in the Holy Spirit, the Lord, the giver of
    life,
    who proceeds from the Father and the Son.
    With the Father and the Son He is worshiped
    and glorified.

He has spoken through the Prophets.
We believe in one holy catholic and apostolic
Church.
We acknowledge one baptism for the forgiveness
of sins.
We look for the resurrection of the dead,
and the life of the world to come. AMEN.

The Nicene Creed doesn't attempt to explain the Trinity. Rather, it presents the ancient truth that runs through the pages of the Bible and the history of the church. This truth cannot be fully explained, but it must be believed. Millard Erickson concluded his treatment of the Trinity by saying:

> [The Trinity] is so absurd from a human standpoint that no one would have invented it. We do not hold the doctrine of the Trinity because it is self-evident or logically cogent. We hold it because God has revealed this is what he is like. As someone has said of this doctrine:
>> Try to explain it, and you'll lose your mind;
>> But try to deny it, and you'll lose your soul.[7]

To this we can only say, amen.

QUESTIONS

When did God make everything?

In the seventeenth century, Anglican archbishop James Ussher calculated the age of the earth using Middle Eastern and Mediterranean histories, along with the genealogies and chronologies found in the Bible. By his estimation, God started creating the heavens and the earth on October 23, 4004 BC. He also calculated that Adam and Eve were driven out of the Garden of Eden eighteen days later, on November 10 of the same year, and that Noah's ark touched down on Mount Ararat on Wednesday, May 5, 2348 BC.

By Ussher's calculation, the universe is now slightly more than six thousand years old. The average science class teaches the universe is a little older — around 10 billion years older — and that the earth is between 4 and 5 billion years old. To be fair, Ussher lived before the birth of modern geology and astronomy, both of which played major roles in the current estimates of the earth's age. His estimates weren't just a churchman's attempt to force biblical views upon the culture as a whole. He worked with the best evidence available to him at the time to answer a question that continues to be answered in a wide variety of ways.

Christians stand apart from naturalists, who believe the universe is the product of natural forces working through the laws of physics without any outside interference.[8] The Bible declares that God made everything — it didn't make itself. Yet even within the community of believers, emotions run high when talk turns to the age of the earth. In the beginning God created the heavens and the earth, but how long ago was "the beginning"? When did God make everything, and how long did the creative process take? Embedded within the question is another: *How did God make everything?* The answers to these questions usually fall within four general schools of thought.[9]

Young Earth Creationism

Young earth creationism (YEC) is the belief that the earth and the rest of creation are between six and ten thousand years old. YEC begins with a very literal approach to the Bible, especially the first few chapters of Genesis. In this view, the six days of creation in Genesis 1 were exactly that — six literal, consecutive, twenty-four-hour days. Believers in YEC cite the common meaning of the Hebrew term יוֹם (*yom*) as evidence. In most usages in the Old Testament, the term refers to a single day. Because this is the normal meaning of the word, YEC supporters see no need to seek another meaning.

Like James Ussher, YEC proponents arrive at an estimate for the earth's age by using the biblical genealogies and chronologies. According to this school of thought, God intends for the Bible to be used this way. In his book *Faith, Form, and Time*, Dr. Kurt Wise argued, "Scripture seems to be designed in such a way that a biblical chronology can be constructed from it. . . . Ultimately, all Christian doctrine is based upon the clear understanding of Scripture and the biblical chronology derived from it. *The nature of the God of creation requires acceptance of biblical chronology and the rejection of conventional old-age chronology.*"[10] For those who hold this view, the issue is more than a supernaturalist view of the universe as opposed to a naturalist one. Believing God created the heavens and the earth also means belief in a young earth.

One of the objections most often raised against this view is the appearance of age that fills nature. From the miles of sedimentary layers geologists encounter to the extreme distance of stars whose light is visible on earth, critics contend that a face-value examination of the evidence shows the earth is millions, if not billions, of years old. YEC proponents don't argue the point. Instead, they maintain that God made the universe with the appearance of age. Just as Adam and Eve were created as adults, not infants, YEC advocates hold that God made a mature universe. That's why the light from stars that are billions of light-years from earth is visible today. God not only created the stars, but he also created the beam of light shining from the star to the earth, thus making it visible from the day it was made. In addition, they say the layers of sediment were laid down during the worldwide flood that occurred during Noah's lifetime.

Young earth creationists are not simply religious zealots with no science background. John Morris, the head of one of the largest YEC organizations, the Institute for Creation Research, holds a PhD in geological engineering from the University of Oklahoma. Many of the leading proponents of YEC have similar backgrounds, including Kurt Wise, who received an MA and a PhD in paleontology from Harvard.

Theistic Evolution

Theistic evolutionists believe God created the universe using natural processes through evolution. Unlike naturalist evolution, Theistic evolutionists do not believe the universe sprang out of nothing. God spoke the universe into existence and continues to work from within through evolutionary processes. While new species evolved from more primitive life-forms, the process was not random. God directs the evolutionary path so that creation can still be called evidence of God's design. Many holding this view leave room for some direct creative act whereby God modified a living creature, giving it a soul or a spiritual nature.[11] This, they say, is how man came to take on the image of God. They agree with the naturalist's position that the earth is millions if not billions of years old. Theistic evolutionists have a more difficult time explaining the very specific creation account in the Bible.

Critics argue that theistic evolution is little more than a position of compromise between the world of science and belief in the Bible. While that charge may be valid, this view can't be wholly dismissed in this way. Many conservative theologians over the past hundred years have held this position, including C. S. Lewis. For Lewis, this wasn't an issue of primary importance. He wrote, "I believe Christianity can still be believed even if evolution is true."[12] Famed theologian B. B. Warfield championed biblical authority while also holding this view. For him, the issue wasn't compromise, but rather, discerning how God created the heavens and the earth. Warfield believed all truth was God's truth, and he was willing to explore the scientific claims supporting evolution to see if they were indeed true, and therefore, evidence of the way God created the universe.[13]

Age-Day Theory

In our usage, age-day theory is an umbrella term for those who believe in the literal truth of the biblical creation account, but who believe the earth is much older than six thousand years. This is sometimes referred to as old earth creationism. While proponents of this view admit the Hebrew word for *day* usually refers to a twenty-four-hour period of time, it doesn't always have this meaning.

Age-day offers alternative answers to some key questions with which young earth creationism struggles, while also taking a more literal approach to the Bible than theistic evolution. For example, questions persist as to how the first three days of creation in Genesis can be twenty-four-hour periods, because a day marks the time it takes the earth to make one complete rotation in relation to the sun. Yet the sun wasn't created until day four, making a literal day impossible. In the same way, when God tells the ground to sprout plants that then grow to maturity and bear fruit on day three, more than twenty-four hours would be needed for this to occur. Also, confining the days of creation to literal days makes day six very action-packed. Adam was created, named all the animals, and then realized his deep need for a companion like him, so God made Eve, all in this final day. Age-day theory sees each of these ambiguities as evidence that the days of creation took place over an extended period rather than in twenty-four-hour periods.

Age-day theory has some heavyweight proponents, including the late Francis Schaeffer, one of the greatest Christian apologists of the twentieth century. He wrote:

> The simple fact is that *day* in Hebrew (just as in English) is used in three separate senses, to mean: (1) twenty-four hours, (2) the period of light during the twenty-four hours, and (3) an indeterminate period of time. Therefore, we must leave open the exact length of time indicated by *day* in Genesis. From the study of the word in Hebrew, it is not clear which way it is to be taken; it could be either way. In the light of the word as used in the Bible and the lack of finality of science concerning the problem of dating, in a sense there is no debate, because there are no clearly defined terms upon which to debate.[14]

Schaeffer's approach shifts the debate over the origins of the universe back to the naturalist versus the supernaturalist view, rather than fighting within the Christian family.

This shift keeps many within this camp from being easily identified with one of the subgroups within this category, such as progressive creationists and proclamation-day creationists, which we will discuss in a moment. Instead, age-day theorists stand out for maintaining the truth that God created the heavens and the earth. As a result, they don't share the young earth creationists' aversion to one of the key components of secular science's explanation for the creation of the cosmos: the big bang theory.

Kurt Wise called the big bang theory "the most popular atheistic theory for the origin of the universe."[15] He even listed a series of reasons why it cannot be correct. However, Christian apologist Charles Colson hailed the big bang theory as a major shift toward the Genesis account of creation when he wrote,

> The truth is that the big bang theory gives dramatic support to the biblical teaching that the universe had an ultimate beginning—that space, matter, and time itself are finite. Far from being a challenge to Christian faith . . . the theory actually gives startling evidence *for* the faith.[16]

Two major explanations for the age of the universe and the way God created it fall within this age-day theory. The first, *progressive creationism*, is the belief that God created everything in a series of acts over an extended period of time. On each of the biblical "days" of creation, God made the first of each "kind" of creature. These kinds may have been as broad as an order or as narrowly focused as a genus or even a species. The first of each "kind" then developed into other species through evolution. This would be similar to the development of the two to four hundred breeds of dog from the wolf. Gaps exist between these different kinds of animals, so there are naturally missing links between huge evolutionary leaps. The entire process stretched out over a very long time, which may have been as long as millions or even billions of years.

The second view is *proclamation-day creationism.* This view says God created the universe in six days, which could well have been as short as twenty-four-hour periods. However, the results of each day stretched out over a much longer period of time, and the days themselves did not immediately follow one another. On each of the six days, God made a proclamation that ordered creation into existence. Then he stepped back and allowed this proclamation to flourish and reach its full result before issuing the next proclamation. Therefore, the first proclamation, "Let there be light," may well have resulted in the explosion of light known as the big bang. God then allowed the raw materials he unleashed in that explosion to spread before he issued the next creative order. The universe and the earth would then be very old, perhaps billions of years, yet they were still created by special acts of God.

Gap Theory

An older attempt to reconcile science with the Bible while also answering the question of the age of the earth is known as the gap theory. This theory, which was espoused by staunch biblical inerrantists such as the late W. A. Criswell, holds that Genesis 1 actually gives two creation accounts. The first is found in Genesis 1:1, where God created the heavens and the earth. According to this view, this original creation was pristine and lasted for a very long time, thus accounting for the geological strata and the distance to visible stars. However, this pristine state did not last. Something, usually attributed to the fall of Satan, spoiled this creation, rendering it empty and void. Genesis 1:2, therefore, describes this state when it says, "The earth was empty, a formless mass cloaked in darkness. And the Spirit of God was hovering over its surface." How much time passed between the first creation and God's rehabilitation of it no one knows. However, once God started recreating the heavens and the earth, he completed the process in six days, just as the Bible says.

The gap theory gained widespread acceptance when it was included in one of the first study Bibles, the Scofield Reference Bible. However, by the end of the twentieth century, it had faded from popularity.

How can God be good with so much bad in the world?

A series of car bombs killed hundreds on the other side of the globe, while in local news, the parents of a young girl who was sexually abused for four years, beginning when she was only six years old, were outraged when the judge sentenced the molester to only sixty days in jail for the crime. In Florida, a gang of young men with baseball bats beat three homeless men, killing one and seriously injuring the other two. A country the president of the United States once called a part of the "axis of evil" moved closer to developing nuclear weapons. Violence continued in the Middle East. Meanwhile, far from the public eye, the death toll climbed as fighting continued unabated in spite of a UN-imposed ceasefire in the Sudan. Experts estimate that as many as 180,000 have died since fighting broke out three years earlier.

All of this happened on a rather slow news day one January. How can a good God stand by and do nothing about everyday events like these, let alone faith-shattering events such as 9/11 and the Holocaust? Even if we can find a way to explain the acts of cruelty people let loose on one another, how can we reconcile the goodness of God with the suffering unleashed by nature? Where was God during the December 2004 tsunami that killed hundreds of thousands of people, or during the killer hurricane season of 2005? Would a good God really allow Hurricane Katrina to wipe out New Orleans and the Gulf Coast? The questions really boil down to two key faith issues: the problem of evil and the problem of pain.

Why Does Evil Exist?

"Is God willing to prevent evil, but not able? Then he is impotent. Is he able, but not willing? Then he is malevolent. Is he both able and willing? Whence then is evil?" The philosopher Epicurus posed these questions nearly three hundred years before the birth of Jesus.[17] Skeptics continue to ask the same questions today. Why would a good God permit evil?

Before exploring the question from the standpoint of believers, it's important to understand that the question raises even more problems for unbelievers and skeptics. Those who throw out the problem of evil as proof that God doesn't exist, or that he is somehow less than the Bible makes him out to be, do so at their own risk. Why? When God is removed from the equation, we come face-to-face with the problem of human evil. The question then goes, "If people are good, why is there evil in the world?" The cruelty found in the human race is unmatched anywhere else in nature. Some animals may eat their young, but they don't develop thermonuclear warheads capable of exterminating everything on the planet many times over.

But that's only the tip of the iceberg. If God and universal, absolute truths do not exist, then all questions of good and evil are nothing more than matters of taste and perception. One man's evil is another man's good. Every act of violence, every infliction of physical or emotional harm, every act against which societies have rules, must have some natural explanation based on evolutionary history. It's hard to imagine an evolutionary reason for a sexual predator brutalizing a small child just for the thrill of it. And if such a person were simply acting out urges programmed deep inside of him by biology and his particular genetic makeup, how can he be held responsible for what he has done?

All of this simply means the problem of evil does not go away if God is removed from the equation. Quite the opposite. Christian theology confronts this problem head-on and offers a credible answer.

The fact that human beings struggle with this problem indicates at least an inkling that something is inherently wrong with the world in which we live. The Bible says this problem is sin, and its consequences run amuck (see Romans 5:12). We will explore sin and its effects on human beings in a later chapter. But for now, suffice it to say that people do cruel things to one another because they have chosen sin over God—that is, they've chosen to reject God's standards in favor of doing whatever they please. Why would God let this happen? The only other choice is to create beings with no choice in how they live their lives. God could have made the human race incapable of doing evil, and then the entire species would be forced to do the right thing at all times. In short, we would not have a free will.

Human beings weren't the only creatures God made with a free will. Although the Bible doesn't go into many details, apparently the angels were also given a choice as to whether they would serve God or reject him outright. Satan and his demons are angels who rebelled against God's authority and were thrown out of heaven (see Revelation 12). The Bible makes it clear that Satan is not equal to God. His power is limited (see Job 1–2), even though he exercises considerable influence in the physical world (see John 12:31, where Jesus calls him "the prince of this world"). Ultimately, God will bind and throw the Devil and his demons into a lake of fire for all eternity (see Revelation 20:10).

Evil is therefore a result of God's giving self-aware creatures a choice as to whether they will serve or reject him. The extent of evil we see in the world indicates that there are no limits to how deep the human race can sink. The suffering humans inflict upon innocent parties is the price we pay for living in a world where we have a free will. That statement may seem coldhearted, but what other options are there? The real problem of evil is a problem that lies in the human soul. "We refine cruelty to an art form and then wonder why God allows it to continue."[18]

The Bible makes it clear that a day is coming when God will put an end to evil once and for all. Revelation 19 says Jesus will return to earth one day to lay waste all of God's enemies and to establish his reign of justice and righteousness on the earth. People wonder why God doesn't do something about the condition of the world. The Bible reassures us that he will. The delay is actually an act of his grace. "The Lord isn't really being slow about his promise to return, as some people think," Peter wrote. "No, he is being patient for your sake. He does not want anyone to perish, so he is giving more time for everyone to repent" (2 Peter 3:9).

Why Is There Pain?

"Here on earth you will have many trials and sorrows," Jesus told his disciples. "But take heart," he continued, "because I have overcome the world" (John 16:33). His words shouldn't have come as a surprise to his disciples, because the prophets had said he would be a "man of sorrows, acquainted with bitterest grief" (Isaiah 53:3). Paul told the church in Philippi, "For you have been given not only the privilege of trusting in Christ but also the privilege of suffering for him" (Philippians 1:29). "Consider it pure joy . . . whenever you face trials of many kinds," James said (James 1:2, NIV). Peter echoed James when he wrote, "Dear friends, don't be surprised at the fiery trials you are going through, as if something strange were happening to you. Instead, be very glad—because these trials will make you partners with Christ in his suffering, and afterward you will have the wonderful joy of sharing his glory when it is displayed to all the world" (1 Peter 4:12-13). Pain, it appears, does not trouble God. It does, however, trouble us.

The verses cited above are but a small sampling of the many passages that speak of pain and suffering. Do not misconstrue the Bible's message and conclude that God commands us to embrace hardship with a smile and a stiff upper lip. The book of Job explores the depths of emotions we feel when we suffer. Many people find Job's outbursts surprising, even theologically wrong. Yet at the end of the book, God commended Job for his faithfulness. We find similar outbursts of sorrow and anger in Jeremiah. Like Job, Jeremiah stands out as an example of one who persevered faithfully under intense pressure, even though he yelled at God in anguish (see Jeremiah 20).

The Bible speaks honestly of pain and suffering, but it never makes excuses for their presence in the world. Suffering exists in this world for the same reason evil exists: It is one of the consequences of sin. Romans 5:12 says that sin brought death into the world. Plants and animals may well have died before sin entered the world, but the death system with its suffering and grief did not exist prior to Adam and Eve's act of disobedience. That doesn't mean that every time you suffer some hardship, God is paying you back for something you've done wrong. Job's comforters thought God operated that way, and they were shown to be wrong. Instead, pain exists because we now live in a fallen world where death and decay are the rule, not the exception.

Does this imply that human sin is responsible for killer hurricanes and all other natural disasters? Not necessarily. Storms and earthquakes and volcanoes are a vital part of the earth's ecosystem. The same flood that causes such despair in those whose homes are washed away also deposits nutrients into the ground, making the ground more fertile when the floods subside. God built a rhythm into the natural world. Many disasters can be avoided by simply learning to pay attention to them. In 1980, a man named Harry Truman refused to leave his cabin in the mountains of Washington just because a nearby volcano had become active. Harry and his beloved cabin were vaporized when Mount St. Helens exploded a few weeks later. His sin didn't cause the volcano to erupt, but his pride and stubbornness led to his demise.

Suffering, whatever its cause, is not pointless to the believer. George MacDonald once said, "The Son of God suffered unto death, not that men might not suffer, but that their sufferings might be like His."[19] This is where Christianity heralds the power of God in the midst of human tragedy. Jesus came and shared our sufferings. Now, for his children, God promises in the Bible that he is able to use even the most tragic events for his ultimate purposes. Paul wrote, "And we know that God causes everything to work together for the good of those who love God and are called according to his purpose for them." As Joseph told his brothers after they sold him into slavery, what the world may intend for evil, God can and will use for our good (see Romans 8:28).[20]

Is God Still in Control?

Knowing why evil and pain exist still leaves us with the question of how God can be all-powerful while allowing suffering and evil to run rampant in the world. Several answers have been proposed.

One solution redefines evil as good. Proponents of this hyper-Calvinist position place an extreme emphasis on God's sovereignty. Because he rules over both the seen and unseen universes, nothing can happen without God's approval. If a sparrow can't fall to the ground without God taking notice, how can anything escape his notice? But he does more than notice. This view teaches that God causes all things to happen. Since everything God does is good, every event that takes place on earth must ultimately be good.

On the opposite end of the spectrum is a view that concludes the reason God doesn't do more about evil in the world is because he cannot. Deemed the "open view of God" or the "open view of the future," this position teaches that God created a world with real freedom for its inhabitants—freedom he will not violate. Moreover, God took a huge risk in creating this world, because, according to this view, he has chosen not to know exactly what will happen. He doesn't foresee or predetermine events unfolding on earth. Rather, all things simply result from the physical laws and human freedom God built into the system. God would do something about evil and suffering if he could. Yet the system he has created, and the uncertainties of an unforeseen future, keep him from doing so.

Another approach to evil and suffering is found in what is normally referred to in American Christianity as the health-and-wealth movement, or the prosperity gospel. This view also places a great deal of emphasis on God's power. This view teaches that he is so powerful that if Christians will exercise enough faith, God will shield them from the effects of living in a fallen world. Material prosperity and physical health are available for every believer. Teachers in this movement point to Isaiah 53:5 to show that Jesus secured divine healing for us when he died and rose again. They also refer to Old Testament promises to Israel regarding the blessings of the Promised Land as further proof that God will counteract the effects of evil in our day-to-day lives, giving us prosperity instead.

A more traditional view of evil and pain and the lordship of God sees God as truly on his throne in heaven. He does not cause evil (see James 1:13), nor does he find pleasure in the suffering of his children. However, God's power is such that he is able to work through the fallen world system to accomplish his ultimate purposes. As mentioned above, God will one day destroy the power of evil once and for all when Christ returns. Until that day, he continues to direct the course of history toward his ultimate end (see Revelation 12). He protects and delivers his children. However, as the book of Job shows, sometimes God allows us to go through times of suffering. Yet even those times work to bring him glory.

How can God be in control and people still be free?

If God is the sovereign Ruler over the universe, how can people still be free? Put another way, do human beings have free will, or are all of our decisions predetermined by God's overarching plan that runs through history?

This question isn't confined to theology. Philosophers have debated the question of free will versus determinism for millennia. Even when God is left out of the debate, the question still remains: Do people possess a true free will, or are all of our actions predetermined by forces outside of our control? This question is central to the plot of *The Matrix* trilogy. Neo fought to make people more than cogs in the machine that was the universe. Yet even then he found himself a prisoner of fate. The Keymaker said in *The Matrix Reloaded*, "We do only what we are meant to do."

Is this true?

As Christians, this question speaks to our fundamental understanding of God and the way he works in the world. Does his rule exercise complete, sovereign control over every decision made by every creature? How much room does he leave for freedom of choice? And if humans have free wills, what impact does this make on God's ability to accomplish his plans on the earth? Can we frustrate or hold God's plans hostage?

A Sovereign God

The Bible appears to present God as absolutely sovereign over all of creation. "Do not forget the things I have done throughout history. For I am God—I alone! I am God, and there is no one else like me," God declared through Isaiah.

"Only I can tell you what is going to happen even before it happens. *Everything I plan will come to pass, for I do whatever I wish*" (Isaiah 46:9-10, emphasis added). God backed this declaration up in the Old Testament as he raised up kings and nations at key times to accomplish his plans. When the Assyrian army demanded that Jerusalem surrender or be destroyed, God told the Assyrian king Sennacherib, "But have you not heard? It was I, the LORD, who decided this long ago. Long ago I planned what I am now causing to happen" (2 Kings 19:25). The idea that God rules over all the events of history is repeated in the New Testament. Paul wrote, "All things happen just as he decided long ago" (Ephesians 1:11).

God doesn't just foreordain the events of history. Romans 9 describes how he works out his plan in and through the lives of individuals. Paul pointed to the lives of Jacob and Esau as he wrote, "But before they were born, before they had done anything good or bad, she received a message from God. (This message proves that God chooses according to his own plan, not according to our good or bad works.) She was told, 'The descendants of your older son will serve the descendants of your younger son.' In the words of the Scriptures, 'I loved Jacob, but I rejected Esau'" (Romans 9:11-13). God's plan even extends to the lives of unbelievers. Through Moses, God told Pharaoh, "I have let you live for this reason — that you might see my power and that my fame might spread throughout the earth" (Exodus 9:16). As Paul said, "So you see, God shows mercy to some just because he wants to, and he chooses to make some people refuse to listen" (Romans 9:18).

All of this seems incredibly unfair to most of us. We ask, in the words of Romans 9:19, "Why does God blame people for not listening? Haven't they simply done what he made them do?" God's answer may surprise you:

> No, don't say that. Who are you, a mere human being, to criticize God? Should the thing that was created say to the one who made it, "Why have you made me like this?" When a potter makes jars out of clay, doesn't he have a right to use the same lump of clay to make one jar for decoration and another to throw garbage into? God has every right to exercise his judgment and his power, but he also has the right to be very patient with those who are the objects of his judgment and are fit only for destruction. He also has the right to pour out the riches of his glory upon those he prepared to be the objects of his mercy — even upon us, whom he selected, both from the Jews and from the Gentiles. (Romans 9:20-24)

What Paul seems to have said in this passage is that since God is God, he can do anything he wants with anyone, and we have no right to complain. He is God, after all. And one of the perks of being God is you can do anything you want and you don't have to answer to anyone.

Based solely on passages like these, the question of God's sovereignty and human free will seems to have an easy answer: God is God and we aren't. He directs the lives of both individuals and nations through the flow of history, and there's not much we can do about it. In the words of the NIV translation of Romans 9:19, who can resist his will? Obviously no one.

Human Free Will

But God's sovereign control of the universe is only part of the picture the Bible paints. Alongside God's sovereignty we see a strong statement on human freedom. Simply put, God gives people a choice in what they will do, and he has done so since the beginning of time. When he placed the first man and woman in the Garden of Eden, he also gave them a simple command: "You may freely eat any fruit in the garden except fruit from the tree of the knowledge of good and evil. If you eat of its fruit, you will surely die" (Genesis 2:16-17). The presence of the tree in the garden means God gave them a choice. Adam and Eve weren't forced to serve the Lord. God didn't create robots, but rather free moral agents with a real ability to choose. When these free moral agents made the wrong choice, they suffered the consequences, albeit with God's promise of forgiveness and restoration built in.

The same pattern continues throughout the Bible. God called out to people, inviting them to enter into a relationship with him, and then he waited patiently for them to turn to him. Eventually his patience ran out, as in the Flood during the days of Noah. But even after he threatened to send punishment, he relented if people repented. God's dealings with the Assyrians in the book of Jonah are a classic example of this. Jonah went to the Assyrian capital, Nineveh, to announce that God's judgment was coming. However, when the people of Nineveh heard the warnings, they all turned to God. When the Lord saw their broken hearts, he showed them mercy and forgave their sins. This ticked off Jonah, who wanted to see fire fall from the sky onto the Assyrians. He complained, "I knew that you were a gracious and compassionate God, slow to get angry and filled with unfailing love" (Jonah 4:2).

Not only does this episode show God's grace and compassion; it also shows how he responds to the choices people make. In the Old Testament Law, he promised to bless the people if they obeyed and to curse them if they turned to other gods. In the New Testament, Jesus promised to forgive anyone who called on his name. As John wrote, "For God so loved the world that he gave his one and only Son, that whoever believes in him shall not perish but have eternal life" (John 3:16, NIV).

In John 3:16, whoever means whoever, without restrictions. That's why Jesus sent his disciples into the entire earth preaching the gospel. His invitation is open to all. Revelation 22:17 says, "Whoever is thirsty, let him come; and whoever wishes, let him take the free gift of the water of life" (NIV). Everyone who hears and responds to Jesus' invitation is forgiven, but those who refuse to believe are condemned. John explained, "God did not send his Son into the world to condemn it, but to save it. There is no judgment awaiting those who trust him. But those who do not trust him have already been judged for not believing in the only Son of God" (John 3:17-18).

These invitations, along with the blessings of believing and the consequences for unbelief, all seem to indicate that people have the ability, the free will, to respond. Simply put: How can a choice be a choice if someone else has already made it for you? And if someone else makes the decision for you, how can you be held responsible for what they have chosen?

Reconciling the Irreconcilable

How can human beings be free and God be sovereign? The answer to this question has historically gone in two directions, which, since the Reformation, have come under the umbrellas of Calvinism and Arminianism, so named for John Calvin (1509–1564) and James Arminius (1560–1609). Calvin, the father of Reformed theology, emphasized God's sovereignty. He taught that Adam, the first man, did indeed have a free will. However, when Adam chose sin instead of God, he and all his descendants lost their freedom of will. Citing Augustine, Calvin said human free will is now held captive by sin. We might have once been free, but we are no longer.[21]

The idea of the bondage of the will to sin is a central part of the theological system derived from Calvin's work. Because human free will is held in bondage by sin, people will not turn to Jesus unless God turns them (see John 6:44,65). Therefore, people do not choose God; he chooses them unconditionally (see Ephesians 1:4-5). He then draws his chosen ones to himself with a grace they cannot resist (see John 6:37). This also means salvation cannot be lost, since it comes as a gift from God given to those he chooses (see John 10:28-29). Some Calvinists also emphasize God's sovereignty to the point of arguing that if Jesus died for every person who had ever lived, everyone would be saved. But because God's intent in giving his Son was to save those he had chosen, Jesus' atonement, the payment he paid for our sins, was limited to those whom God had chosen before the foundation of the world.

These main points of Calvinism have been reduced to the acrostic TULIP, which stands for:

> Total depravity of man.
> Unconditional election.
> Limited atonement.
> Irresistible grace.
> Perseverance of the saints.

James Arminius, a Dutch reformer, answered the question of God's sovereignty and human freedom by placing his primary emphasis on the latter. Writing in response to Calvinism, he started with the premise that God wants all people to be saved (see 1 Timothy 2:4). He agreed with Calvin regarding the sinfulness of the entire human race. However, he taught that God had extended his grace to the entire world, enabling them to respond to the gospel (see John 12:32; 16:8). Like Calvin, he emphasized that God chooses who will be saved. However, Arminius taught that God's election is based on his foreknowledge of who will accept Christ. Therefore, God's grace can be rejected, because people face a real choice when they hear the gospel (see Hebrews 4:2-3). Most Arminians believe salvation can be forfeited if one chooses to stop believing in Jesus (see Hebrews 2:1-4). Arminius also rejected the idea that Jesus' atoning work was in any way limited. The Son of God died for the entire world, although only those who believe will be saved (see John 3:16).

How then can man be free and God be in control? Calvinists say man cannot be free, for God is in complete control. Arminians say God has limited the control he exercises to make room for human freedom. Which is correct? Strict adherents try to make this an either/or question. However, most believers fall somewhere in between, either leaning more to one side than the other.

Jesus

ESSENTIALS

God in Flesh

Jesus and the Cross

Prophet, Priest, and King

QUESTIONS

When will Jesus come back, and what will happen when he does?

The unknown graffiti artist laughed to himself as he scratched the picture into the wall. On one side he drew a man with a donkey's head hanging on a cross. Slightly below and to the left he drew another man with one hand raised as though in prayer. Below the picture he scrawled:

ΑΛΕ

ΧΑΜΕΝΟΣ

ΣΕΒΕΤΕ

ΘΕΟΝ

That is, Alexamenos worships [his] god.[1]

The first- or second-century tagger never imagined his little joke would survive more than eighteen hundred years. Yet the Alexamenos Graffito continues to summarize both the great mystery and the great stumbling block that is Christianity. How could God hang on a cross? And why would anyone in his right mind worship as god a man hung naked on a cross, executed as a criminal by the Roman government? Paul was correct when he said, "The Message that points to Christ on the Cross seems like sheer silliness to those hellbent on destruction, but for those on the way of salvation it makes perfect sense. This is the way God works, and most powerfully as it turns out" (1 Corinthians 1:18, MSG).

The very thought of God on a cross would seem like sheer silliness if it were not true. Yet this is the centerpiece of our faith. Christianity is all about Jesus. And who Jesus is cannot be separated from what he came to earth to do, all of which brings us back to Alexamenos worshiping his God. The One mocked in a crudely drawn graffito on an ancient Roman wall is what this faith is all about. He is the One in whom we have placed our hope.

ESSENTIALS

God in Flesh

The twelve disciples had just witnessed the kind of miracles no one had even imagined possible since the days of Elisha. Yet not even Elisha on his best day did anything like what Jesus now made an everyday occurrence. Twice he'd fed huge crowds with next to nothing. He'd opened the eyes of the blind and even raised the dead. Try as they might, the twelve couldn't shake the fear that swept over them when they saw Jesus strolling across the Sea of Galilee while a storm raged. After the way he had told a storm to stop and it obeyed him, they knew Jesus' power knew no limits.

Maybe that's why Jesus' question took them aback. Of course they'd discussed his question among themselves many, many times, but never when Jesus was around. "Who do you say I am?" he asked. They all knew what they wanted to say. All of them felt it. Jesus had to be the Messiah, the Christ, the Savior about whom the prophets had written. Yet putting these thoughts into words seemed somehow wrong. The Jews had waited so long for God's promised Deliverer, and through the centuries so many fake Christs had come on the scene that most of the Twelve hesitated to speak. Finally Peter blurted out what the rest of them were thinking: "You are the Messiah, the Son of the living God" (Matthew 16:15-16).

Two thousand years later we've grown so accustomed to the idea that Jesus is the Christ that we have trouble understanding the weight of that moment. Yet the question needs to be asked again, because so many people paint so many different pictures of Jesus. There's the cultural Jesus—the lovey-dovey, wouldn't hurt a fly, wouldn't say a cross word to anyone, sweet and syrupy caricature of Jesus. Then there's the Jesus of the fire-and-brimstone preachers, who inflicts world leaders with fatal diseases for going against his will. Then there's the movie Jesus, the one who talks with an English accent and seems more like a first-century flower child than the Savior of the world. And finally, there's the wristband Jesus, the W.W.J.D.? Jesus. He's not as popular as he once was. Lance Armstrong's yellow, rubber bracelets knocked him off of most wrists. Still, for a while, everyone asked what he would do, although many of those wearing the bracelets engaged in behavior that didn't exactly seem like anything Jesus might do.

So who is Jesus? He is the One in whom God and man come together in a way that his harshest critics, the Pharisees, could never understand.

God

The answer to the question of who Jesus is begins here. He is fully God. Long before his birth, Isaiah called him Immanuel, which means "God with us" (see Isaiah 7:14). The prophet also told us who this coming Messiah would be when he wrote, "For a child is born to us, a son is given to us. And the government will rest on his shoulders. These will be his royal titles: Wonderful Counselor, *Mighty God*, *Everlasting Father*, Prince of Peace" (Isaiah 9:6, emphasis added). Assigning such titles to a mere human being would be the worst form of blasphemy, but Jesus wasn't merely a man. He was God-made-flesh.

The New Testament presents Jesus as fully God from beginning to end. In Matthew and Luke, the angels announce his birth, declaring that the baby born in a manger is Immanuel. The Father's voice booms from heaven at his baptism: "This is my beloved Son" (Matthew 3:17). In Jesus' day, to claim God as one's personal Father was tantamount to claiming equality with God. Jesus didn't have to make this claim (although he did so repeatedly). His Father did it for him. We see Jesus' deity through his miracles, and especially in his authority over all the forces of nature. He revealed his glory to Peter, James, and John on top of a mountain, where once again the Father spoke up on his Son's behalf. Jesus knew who he was when he forgave sins and allowed people to worship him. Then there was the greatest proof of all—his resurrection from the dead.

The New Testament explicitly tells us that Jesus is fully God. Nowhere is this clearer than the first sentence of John's gospel: "In the beginning was the Word, and the Word was with God, and the Word was God" (John 1:1, NIV). In verse 14 John added, "The Word became flesh and made his dwelling among us. We have seen his glory, the glory of the One and Only, who came from the Father, full of grace and truth." Those who try to deny Christ's deity try to add an indefinite article to verse one, making it read, "and the Word was a god."[2] Yet the way the verse is written in the original language doesn't allow this. A literal, word-for-word translation reads, "And God was the Word."

John expanded on this idea in the verses that follow. He told how all things were created through Jesus, going so far as to say that nothing was created apart from him. This means Jesus could not have been a created being, because he could not create himself. John also described Jesus' essential Godness when he said, "Life itself was in him, and this life gives light to everyone. The light shines through the darkness, and the darkness can never extinguish it" (John 1:4-5). God alone possesses life in himself independent of anyone or anything. Jesus possesses both life and light, and that light is the light of the world. Writing at a time when Jesus' deity was already coming under attack, John, one of Jesus' closest disciples, wanted to make sure no one missed this vital truth.

Paul also emphasized the deity of Christ. In his letter to the Colossians he wrote:

> Christ is the visible image of the invisible God. He existed before God made anything at all and is supreme over all creation. Christ is the one through whom God created everything in heaven and earth. He made the things we can see and the things we can't see—kings, kingdoms, rulers, and authorities. Everything has been created through him and for him. He existed before everything else began, and he holds all creation together. (Colossians 1:15-17)

Paul also explained how Jesus could be God and yet come to earth as a man. In Philippians 2:6-7 he wrote, "Though he was God, he did not demand and cling to his rights as God. He made himself nothing; he took the humble position of a slave and appeared in human form." Paul even called him "our God and Lord, Jesus Christ" (2 Thessalonians 1:12).

The writer of Hebrews devoted the first chapter of his letter to showing Jesus' supremacy to everything else in creation. He said of him,

> God promised everything to the Son as an inheritance, and through the Son he made the universe and everything in it. The Son reflects God's own glory, and everything about him represents God exactly. He sustains the universe by the mighty power of his command. After he died to cleanse us from the stain of sin, he sat down in the place

of honor at the right hand of the majestic God of heaven.
(Hebrews 1:2-3)

The book of Revelation completes the picture of Christ's
deity. There we find him stepping onto heaven's throne, where
all the host of heaven adore him. At the end of the book, he
returns to earth to receive his kingdom once and for all.

In addition to direct references to Jesus as God, the New
Testament's confession of faith places Jesus and his Father on
equal footing. In the Old Testament, the Israelites were told
that the Lord God is the only true God. In the New, that title
extends to Jesus as well. "Jesus is Lord" became the watch-
word of all believers. Paul wrote in Romans that anyone who
confesses Jesus is Lord will be saved and told the Philippians
that one day "every knee will bow, in heaven and on earth and
under the earth, and every tongue will confess that Jesus Christ
is Lord, to the glory of God the Father" (Philippians 2:10-11).
This confession, he told the church in Corinth, is the distin-
guishing mark of true believers (see 1 Corinthians 12:2-3).

Man

Yet Jesus wasn't just completely God. He was also completely
human. He had to be to do the work his Father sent him here
to do. Jesus wasn't some sort of half-God, half-man mutant.
His humanity did not diminish his divinity, nor did his
divinity diminish his humanity. He was 100 percent God and
100 percent human. As a result, he was able to bridge the gap
between God and people that our sin created. More on that in
the next chapter.

When Jesus laid his glory aside to take on human flesh, he
became like us in every way. He came into the world in the

normal human way. After growing inside his mother for nine months, he was born to a carpenter and his fiancée in a barn in Bethlehem. However, he wasn't conceived in the normal way. His mother was a virgin when he was born. He was conceived through an act of the Holy Spirit sweeping over her. But aside from his conception, everything else about Jesus' life was exactly what you would expect from a flesh-and-bone human being. He felt hunger and thirst, along with the full range of normal human emotions. He cried at the tomb of a close friend and got angry when he saw how the chief priests had allowed the temple to be turned into a religious flea market.

And like the rest of the human race, he felt temptation. However, because he didn't inherit the sin nature passed down from Adam and Eve, he didn't feel the inner compulsion to cheat on a test or punch his brother in the head when his mother wasn't looking. That doesn't mean he was any less tempted than we are. Far from it. Satan himself showed up one day when Jesus was at his weakest point physically. Three times Satan tempted him, going so far as to offer him all the kingdoms of the world. Yet Jesus didn't give in. Instead of calling down fire from the sky to destroy the Devil, Jesus resisted him by quoting the Bible.

The ultimate show of Jesus' humanity came when the Romans tortured and executed him. Again, even though Jesus performed miracles, he wasn't some sort of superman. He felt the physical pain of the whip and the nails, along with the emotional pain of being rejected by both his disciples and his Father. Jesus didn't face the cross like God, but like a man. Death through crucifixion was slow and horrifying. After crying out, "It is finished," he breathed his last breath and died just like every other criminal crucified that day (see John 19:30).

We will explore Jesus' work on the cross in depth in the next chapter. However, for now it's important to understand how his purpose for coming to earth, the reason he became human, was wrapped up in the cross. Jesus had to become fully human to die on the cross in our place. And he had to be fully God for his death to have the power to save every person throughout time who has called and will call on his name.

Moreover, the book of Hebrews tells us that because he is fully God and fully human, he now sits at God's right hand, interceding on our behalf as our great High Priest (see Hebrews 10:12; Romans 8:34). As Hebrews 4:15-16 says, "This High Priest of ours understands our weaknesses, for he faced all of the same temptations we do, yet he did not sin. So let us come boldly to the throne of our gracious God. There we will receive his mercy, and we will find grace to help us when we need it."

The deity and humanity of Jesus isn't just some boring doctrine confined to a theology book. We take this truth for granted every time we call out to Jesus for help. Who he is changes the way we can now approach life. The One who is 100 percent God and 100 percent man now opens the door for us to know God and find grace from him when we need it most.

Jesus and the Cross

Jesus came to die. When the end came, he made it clear that no one took his life from him; he gave it on his own (see John 10:14-18). As we try to understand who Jesus is, we must see everything about him through the lens of his death and what followed. Jesus knew he had a limited time of public ministry. He lived hardly more than three years from the day he was baptized by John the Baptist until he went to the cross. This gives Jesus' teaching an even greater urgency. He didn't waste words. He didn't have time for that. The Son of God came to earth to tell us about his Father, and we need to hang on his every word.

His death also gave Jesus greater authority. What an understatement. It gave him the *ultimate* authority, because he didn't stay dead. When we talk of his death, when we talk about the cross, we refer not only to the way he died, but also to what happened three days later. Jesus died on a cross for our sins, and he rose again bodily to give us life. All he said and did before his death now takes on even greater importance. His words and deeds aren't just those of an itinerant teacher who lived a long time ago. They are the words of the risen Lord of lords. Until we listen to his words against the dark music of the cross, we don't really hear them.

The cross is the focal point of Christianity. Above all our talk of peace and love and reconciliation stands the cross. John Stott said it best: "There is then, it is safe to say, no Christianity without the cross. If the cross is not central to our religion, ours is not the religion of Jesus."[3]

Therefore, to truly understand who Jesus is, we must explore the cross. Our Christology—our theology of Jesus—is a theology of the cross. The two are inseparable. Paul put it this way:

"May I never boast except in the cross of our Lord Jesus Christ, through which the world has been crucified to me, and I to the world" (Galatians 6:14, NIV).

The Perfect Sacrifice

Jesus' path to the cross was paved by the sacrifices demanded by the Old Testament Law. The penalty of sin is now and has always been death. It isn't that those who sin will eventually die. When we sin, we die spiritually. That means our spirits are cut off from God, the Author of life. Our bodies will eventually follow. Yet God's great compassion couldn't leave the human race in these desperate straits. In the Old Testament, an animal's life could be given as a substitute for the life of the sinner. The intricate system outlined in Exodus and Leviticus may be hard to make sense of today, but it foreshadows Jesus' death.

Every Old Testament sacrifice was to be an enacted prayer. Before the worshiper killed the animal and placed it on the altar, the worshiper laid his hands on the animal's head, in effect telling God that the fate that was about to befall this sheep or goat was what the worshiper deserved for his sin. Sacrifices were offered both for individuals and for the nation of Israel as a whole.

God gave specific instructions for the kinds of animals worshipers could offer. Whether a sheep, goat, ox, or dove, the animal had to be physically perfect. People couldn't offer the runt of the litter or some diseased animal that wasn't worth anything anyway. God demanded one of the best animals the people owned. Then, for most sacrifices, the animal's blood was poured out next to the altar and the animal itself burned up completely as an offering to God. Once a year on the Day of Atonement, the high priest carried some sacrificial blood into the Holy of Holies in the temple. He sprinkled it on the cover of the ark of the covenant, which held the Ten Commandments. He did this to remove the guilt for the sins the nation had committed during the previous year.

All of this may seem arcane and irrelevant to your daily life, but the Old Testament sacrificial system set the stage for Jesus' death on the cross. He came to be the final sacrifice for the sins of the entire world. He was, in the words of John the Baptist, the Lamb of God who takes away the sin of the world (see John 1:29). That's why his birth and life were so different from those of an ordinary human being. He was born without the sin nature that has plagued every person born since Adam and Eve ate the forbidden fruit. He was fully human, yet in the way Adam and Eve were before they fell (see Romans 5).

His coming as the final, perfect sacrifice for sins is why it's also so important that he lived a sinless life. Unlike the priests under the sacrificial system, he didn't need to offer a sacrifice for his own sins. Instead, he offered himself. The writer of Hebrews put it this way:

> He is the kind of high priest we need because he is holy and blameless, unstained by sin. He has now been set apart from sinners, and he has been given the highest place of honor in heaven. He does not need to offer sacrifices every day like the other high priests. They did this for their own sins first and then for the sins of the people. But Jesus did this once for all when he sacrificed himself on the cross. (7:26-27)

If Jesus had been merely a sinful human being, his offering of himself would have no effect. But, since he never sinned, he alone did not deserve death, so he could die in our place as our sacrifice for sin.

The sacrifices in the Old Testament had to be repeated year after year. But Jesus' sacrifice was final, an act that never has to be repeated. The effects of what he did will last forever. But what, exactly, did Jesus accomplish through the cross?

Saving Sinners

The simplest, most direct way we can understand the power of the cross is this: God saves sinners through Jesus' death. That's why he came to earth. "For the Son of Man came to seek and to save what was lost," Jesus said in Luke 19:10 (NIV). Paul echoed Jesus when he told Timothy, "This is a true saying, and everyone should believe it: Christ Jesus came into the world to save sinners—and I was the worst of them all" (1 Timothy 1:15).

But what does it mean to be "saved"? The word draws a picture of someone who is in perilous danger, with death closing in quickly. The dying person has nowhere to turn and absolutely no hope of surviving. Suddenly, Jesus reaches down and rescues her. But he does more than deliver us from danger. His death and resurrection save us by destroying those who sought to harm us (see 1 Corinthians 15; Colossians 2:13-15).

From whom and what does Jesus save us? He saves us from the enemies that no one can escape: Satan, sin, and death. The Bible says that in our natural state, we are held captive by Satan to do his will (see 2 Timothy 2:26; Colossians 1:13). Even if Satan relaxed his grip, sin still holds us in its power, strangling us and holding us down until death can finish us off. But, when Jesus died and rose again, he laid waste to all of his enemies. He saved us by setting us free from those who held us captive. Hebrews 2:14-15 says,

Because God's children are human beings—made of flesh and blood—Jesus also became flesh and blood by being born in human form. For only as a human being could he die, and only by dying could he break the power of the Devil, who had the power of death. Only in this way could he deliver those who have lived all their lives as slaves to the fear of dying.

Life

How could Jesus' death rescue us from the fear of dying? Simply put: He didn't stay dead. Three days after the Romans sealed the grave containing his cold, dead body, God raised him from the dead. An angel rolled the stone away from the tomb where he lay, and Jesus walked out of the grave. The soldiers standing guard took one look and fainted. When Mary Magdalene and some of the other women came to the tomb to anoint Jesus' body with spices, they found it was empty. His body wasn't there because he was no longer dead. Over the course of the next forty days, he appeared to the apostles and later to as many as five hundred people at one time. One of the apostles, Thomas, didn't believe Jesus was alive. To make sure Thomas knew it was really him, Jesus invited him to touch the nail prints in his wrists and reach his hand into the place where the spear gouged his side (see John 20).

Jesus didn't just appear to be alive, nor did his memory live on in the hearts of his followers while his body rotted in the ground. He rose from the dead bodily. Paul explained the event to a group of Jews in Antioch:

God's promise to our ancestors has come true in our own time, in that God raised Jesus. This is what the second psalm is talking about when it says concerning Jesus, "You are my Son. Today I have become your Father." For God had promised to raise him from the dead, never again to die. This is stated in the Scripture that says, "I will give you the sacred blessings I promised to David." Another psalm explains more fully, saying, "You will not allow your Holy One to rot in the grave." Now this is not a reference to David, for after David had served his generation according to the will of God, he died and was buried, and his body decayed. No, it was a reference to someone else — someone whom God raised and whose body did not decay. (Acts 13:32-37)

Because Jesus rose from the dead, he now gives life to those who place their hope in him. He said, "I have come that they may have life, and have it to the full" (John 10:10, NIV). Christ doesn't just enhance the quality of our lives today. In him we have real life, eternal life. "I am the resurrection and the life," Jesus said. "He who believes in me will live, even though he dies; and whoever lives and believes in me will never die" (John 11:25-26, NIV). The bodies we have now will wear out, but that's not the end of the story. Just as Jesus rose from the dead, he will raise his followers when he returns. We will then live in his presence forever in bodies freed from the frailties that plague us now. Unlike many religions, Christian theology takes a high view of the human body. The Son of God will have a human body into eternity. We too will live not as disembodied souls, but as persons with bodies. As Paul wrote, "The Spirit of God, who raised Jesus from the dead, lives in you. And just as he raised Christ from the dead, he will give life to your mortal body by this same Spirit living within you" (Romans 8:11). Jesus' resurrection is the guarantee of our own.

Redeeming Slaves of Sin

Not only does Jesus save us; he also redeems us—that is, he buys us back from someone who regards us as his property. The Bible draws a word picture of redemption in the Old Testament book of Hosea. God told Hosea to marry a prostitute, a woman named Gomer. After bearing three children to Hosea, Gomer went back to her old way of life. At some point she sank so low that she became the property of her pimp. God then told Hosea to go and buy her back. But he wasn't just to buy her freedom. Hosea had to take Gomer back as his wife and love her as if nothing had happened.

The Bible tells us that before Jesus comes into our lives, we too are slaves. We live as slaves of sin and slaves of the curse of the Law, which is death. When Jesus died and rose again, he bought us back from our cruel masters. The price he paid was the price of his own life. The Bible tells us we were purchased by his blood (see Ephesians 1:7). We now belong to him. Paul wrote, "You do not belong to yourself, for God bought you with a high price. So you must honor God with your body" (1 Corinthians 6:19-20). Note again that emphasis on our bodies. Just as we were enslaved by our compulsions, most of which involve our bodies, so now we honor God with our bodies, as well as our minds and spirits.

Yet even though God has bought us, he doesn't treat us like slaves. Instead, like Hosea, he loves us, even calling us his bride (see 2 Corinthians 11:2). This is what it means to be redeemed through the power of the cross.

Making the Guilty Innocent

Jesus' work on the cross allows a curious transaction to take place. He died in our place. He paid the penalty of death we deserved because of our sins. This doesn't just earn us a second chance with God. He does something far more radical. Paul explained, "God made him who had no sin to be sin for us, so that in him we might become the righteousness of God" (2 Corinthians 5:21, NIV). By doing so, God makes us innocent by removing every trace of our guilt and shame. We then become holy in his sight.

This may not seem so radical until you consider exactly what it means. God doesn't just forgive our sins. Isaiah 61:10 tells us that God drapes us in a robe of holiness, which Isaiah compared to a bridegroom in his tuxedo or a bride covered with jewels. God declares us not guilty of everything we've ever done—past, present, and future. In his eyes, our lives are as pure as the life of his Son, Jesus. The offense of our sin isn't just removed. We become sinless in God's eyes. It's as though we had never sinned, no matter how ugly our pasts may be.

Forgiving Our Sins

Jesus told a story in Matthew 18 to illustrate the meaning of forgiveness. A man was dragged before a king to whom he owed millions upon millions of dollars with no way to pay it. In keeping with the custom of the day, the king ordered the sale of all the man's possessions and sold the man, his wife, and his children as slaves. The price they would bring wouldn't even begin to pay the debt, but it would bring in more than the man would ever be able to pay. The man fell down before the king and begged for a little more time to pay off the debt. Feeling compassion for the man, the king wiped the debt off the books.

That is what God does for us when he forgives our sins. Many of us feel we've committed only small-time sins, so the news that we've committed capital crimes shocks us. But treason against God, along with the harm we've done to people, deserves the death penalty (see Romans 6:23). Every sin directly targets God. When he made us in his image, he made us to know him, love him, and serve him. Sin is telling our rightful King to take a hike and let us live however we want. Even if we vow to stop sinning and try to live a better life, we've still accumulated a huge debt before God.

When Jesus died in our place, he paid our debt for us. A financial exchange took place, and God marked our bill "paid in full." Colossians 2:13-14 puts it this way: "You were dead because of your sins and because your sinful nature was not yet cut away. Then God made you alive with Christ. He forgave all our sins. He canceled the record that contained the charges against us. He took it and destroyed it by nailing it to Christ's cross." This is what forgiveness means. We no longer stand in debt before God. The offense and guilt of our sin have been taken away forever.

Reconciling Us to God

The other words that describe the cross's effects primarily deal with our sin and guilt. Yet Jesus does more than remove our sinfulness. When the first man and woman sinned, a huge gulf erupted between the entire human race and God. Sin cannot come near God any more than darkness can survive in a room filled with light. Jesus' death and resurrection bridge this gap. Peter wrote, "Christ also suffered when he died for our sins once for all time. He never sinned, but he died for sinners that he might bring us safely home to God" (1 Peter 3:18). In Christ we are reconciled to God.

Once again, the Bible gives us a word picture to help us understand what this means. Jesus told a story about a son who demanded his father give him his share of the family inheritance, which the son promptly went out and blew on "wild living." After he ran out of money, a famine hit the land, and the son found himself starving. Finally he came to his senses and decided to go home. He knew he'd blown his chance with his father but hoped to be hired on as a servant. But when the boy went home, he found his father waiting for him. His father threw a party to celebrate his lost son's return. The father didn't just let the boy back into the house. He restored him and treated him as if nothing had ever come between them (see Luke 15:11-32).

That is how Jesus reconciles us to his Father, who then adopts us into his family and gives us the best he has. The first chapter of Ephesians describes how God has given us every blessing heaven can hold. We become both children of God and heirs of his fortune. Because Jesus reconciled us by taking away the offense of our sin, nothing can ever come between us and God. Paul asked, "What can we say about such wonderful things as these?" His answer:

> If God is for us, who can ever be against us? Since God did not spare even his own Son but gave him up for us all, won't God, who gave us Christ, also give us everything else? . . . And I am convinced that nothing can ever separate us from his love. Death can't, and life can't. The angels can't, and the demons can't. Our fears for today, our worries about tomorrow, and even the powers of hell can't keep God's love away. Whether we are high above the sky or in the deepest ocean, nothing in all creation will ever be able to separate us from the love of God that is revealed in Christ Jesus our Lord. (Romans 8:31-32,38-39)

Prophet, Priest, and King

Three unique sets of leaders guided Old Testament Israel: prophets, priests, and later, kings. Each represented God, guiding his people in their relationship with him. The prophets were God's spokespeople. Priests interceded between the people and God, offering sacrifices through which people found forgiveness. Finally, the king ruled in God's place. He wasn't just a political leader. His job was to discern God's will for the nation and carry it out. The Lord set up Israel to be a theocracy, where ultimately, God himself was King. Prophets, priests, and kings were the human ambassadors through whom God brought his kingdom to earth and into both the life of the nation and the lives of individuals.

When Jesus came to earth, he was the ultimate fulfillment of all three leadership roles, not only for the Jews, but also for the entire world. He was *the* Prophet who didn't just speak *for* God, but *as* God as well. In the same way, he was the greatest and last High Priest, who offered himself as the final sacrifice for sin and now speaks to the Father on our behalves. And he was the true King, who brought his kingdom to earth and continues to reign today. One day in the future he will return to reign visibly over his kingdom once and for all.

These three leadership positions—prophet, priest, and king—are key elements not only of what Jesus came to do two thousand years ago, but also of what he continues to do today. Therefore, understanding these roles and how Jesus acts through them is essential to fully understanding our Savior and his role in our lives today.

Prophet

Biblical prophets were not soothsayers or psychics. They didn't go into trances and foretell the future like mystic oracles. Instead, they spoke for God. At times Old Testament prophets warned God's people of what would happen in the future, yet even then the heart of the message came back to God's longing to draw his people close to him. The warnings of future judgment were all designed to convince the people to turn away from their false gods and sinful ways, back to God.

Moses was Israel's first and greatest prophet. Through him God gave his Law. Moses was so highly respected that during the time of Jesus, a group called the Sadducees refused to acknowledge any other part of the Bible as God's Word except the five books Moses penned. Theirs was a minority view, yet it demonstrates how great Moses was in the Jews' eyes. Moses, however, knew he was but the first prophet. He told the people in his farewell address, "The LORD your God will raise up for you a prophet like me from among your fellow Israelites, and you must listen to that prophet" (Deuteronomy 18:15). These words spoke not only of the string of prophets God later sent, but also of one unique Prophet who would be even greater than Moses.

Jesus came to fulfill this promise. As Peter said in Acts 3:20-22, Jesus is *the* Prophet, not just a prophet. He far exceeds every other spokesperson. Hebrews 1:1-2 explains, "Long ago God spoke many times and in many ways to our ancestors through the prophets. But now in these final days, he has spoken to us through his Son." Jesus speaks *for* God and *as* God. He told his disciples, "Anyone who has seen me has seen the Father!" (John 14:9). Unlike other prophets, he embodies God's message. That's why John's gospel begins, "In the beginning was the Word. . . . And the Word became flesh and made his dwelling among us" (John 1:1,14, NIV). If we want to know what God is like, we need only to look at Jesus.

From the moment Jesus first spoke publicly, all who heard him knew he was unlike anyone else who claimed to speak for God. One of his first messages is found in Luke 4:16-30. What he said set the stage for the rest of the Prophet's ministry. He went to the synagogue on the Sabbath and read from the scroll of Isaiah:

> "The Spirit of the Lord is upon me,
>> for he has appointed me to preach Good News to the poor.
> He has sent me to proclaim
>> that captives will be released,
>> that the blind will see,
>> that the downtrodden will be freed from their oppressors,
>> and that the time of the Lord's favor has come."
> He rolled up the scroll, handed it back to the attendant, and sat down. . . . Then he said, "This Scripture has come true today before your very eyes!" (Luke 4:18-21)

The good news Jesus came to proclaim was news of God's kingdom invading earth. Sight for the blind and release for captives, both spiritual and physical — these were the works of God's kingdom. Jesus did these works during his earthly ministry and told his followers to keep doing them after his resurrection. He urged his hearers to live as citizens of God's kingdom here and now, doing the things the King wants done.

But he didn't just walk around talking about peace and love. The peace he brought was real peace with God, yet it puts a person at odds with the world. He told his followers:

"Don't imagine that I came to bring peace to the earth! No, I came to bring a sword. I have come to set a man against his father, and a daughter against her mother, and a daughter-in-law against her mother-in-law. Your enemies will be right in your own household! If you love your father or mother more than you love me, you are not worthy of being mine; or if you love your son or daughter more than me, you are not worthy of being mine. If you refuse to take up your cross and follow me, you are not worthy of being mine. If you cling to your life, you will lose it; but if you give it up for me, you will find it." (Matthew 10:34-39)

Of course, most people treated Jesus just as they did all the earlier prophets. After he finished preaching the message found in Luke 4, the people tried to push him off a cliff to shut him up. They didn't succeed — that time. But later their leaders rejected his message and urged the Romans to crucify him. The Prophet revealed his Father through both his words and actions, yet the religious leaders accused him of blasphemy. It should therefore come as no surprise when people dismiss his message as nothing but religious nonsense today. However, their failure to listen doesn't diminish his continuing message as the Prophet of God.

Priest

Under the Law of Moses, the priests were in charge of worship and sacrifices at the tabernacle and later the temple. Ordinary people could not approach God directly because of their sin.

The priests went for them, acting as mediators between sinners and God. The regulations for carrying out their duties were detailed, encompassing everything from who qualified for the priesthood to what they must wear and how they must wash before approaching the altar. Only males between the ages of twenty-five and fifty from the tribe of Levi[4] could serve at the temple, and of those, only direct descendants of Moses' brother Aaron could be priests.

Humanly speaking, Jesus did not qualify for the priesthood, because he came from the tribe of Judah, not Levi. However, the book of Hebrews goes into great detail to show how God appointed Jesus as the final High Priest. How did God get around his own requirements? He made his Son a priest like Melchizedek, a mysterious figure from Genesis 14 who served as a priest-king a few hundred years before the Law of Moses came into effect. Hebrews 7:18-19 explains, "Yes, the old requirement about the priesthood was set aside because it was weak and useless. For the law made nothing perfect, and now a better hope has taken its place. And that is how we draw near to God."

Hebrews goes on to say that the tabernacle and temple in Jerusalem were mere copies of the heavenly temple, just as the animal sacrifices foreshadowed something much better. Therefore, when Jesus offered himself as the final sacrifice for sin, he then took his own blood into the Most Holy Place of the heavenly temple and made atonement for our sin once and for all. He then sat down beside his Father and continues to intercede on our behalves. Unlike the human priests whose terms expired at death, Jesus is a Priest forever. This means he will always be beside his Father, continually pleading our case.

Jesus is our Great High Priest, but that doesn't mean the priesthood ended when he ascended into heaven. Peter explained that God has made believers into a "kingdom of priests, God's holy nation, his very own possession. This is so you can show others the goodness of God, for he called you out of the darkness into his wonderful light" (1 Peter 2:9). Like the Old Testament priests, we too are to offer up sacrifices. Instead of sheep or goats, we offer a "sacrifice of praise to God by proclaiming the glory of his name" (Hebrews 13:15).

Jesus makes all of this possible. He removed the barriers that separated us from God and gave us something Old Testament believers never had: direct access to God. As Hebrews 4:15-16 promises, "This High Priest of ours understands our weaknesses, for he faced all of the same temptations we do, yet he did not sin. So let us come boldly to the throne of our gracious God. There we will receive his mercy, and we will find grace to help us when we need it."

King

When God first brought the ancient Israelites into the Promised Land, he didn't give them a king. Instead, he wanted them to stand apart from the rest of the nations on earth. They had tribal leaders, but the Lord himself was Israel's King. He communicated his will through his prophets and the books of Moses. If the people would simply listen and obey, God promised to bless them beyond their wildest dreams. They didn't just have to accept his word on blind faith. All they had to do was think back to the ways he destroyed Egypt when he set them free and how he defeated their enemies when they took possession of the land.

Eventually, however, the people demanded a king they could see. They never fully grasped how to live by faith. God answered their request, giving them Saul, a king who looked the part. His reign ended disastrously. That's when God chose a king after his own heart. When God gave the throne to David of Bethlehem, he promised to extend from David's bloodline a royal dynasty that would last for all time. God vowed to raise up one of David's descendants and establish his throne forever (see 1 Chronicles 17:12).

Eventually Israel split into two small, weak kingdoms. A series of kings who had descended from David governed the southern kingdom, Judah, while kings from various families ruled over the northern kingdom, Israel. Neither kingdom had the strength to last. God's people rejected him and turned to idolatry again and again. Finally, God had enough and sent his people into exile. Seventy years after the Babylonians destroyed Jerusalem, the Jews were allowed to go home. However, they didn't return as an independent nation. The kings never reigned again, and life never again came close to the golden years of David and his son Solomon.

The Jews found hope in the promise God gave David and repeated through the prophets. They looked forward to the return of their King, the Messiah, who would restore the kingdom and usher in a time of God's unlimited blessings.

Jesus fulfilled this promise. He was a direct descendant of King David and therefore a rightful heir to the throne. But, as with his role as our Great High Priest, his reign extends far beyond the borders of one small nation in a corner of the Middle East. Jesus is the King of kings. He rules from heaven's throne over a kingdom that knows no end. This may seem hard to understand, because Jesus was born into poverty and never held political office. The Jews couldn't quite grasp his kingship during his lifetime either. But they thought far too small. As Isaiah promised of Jesus in Isaiah 9:7, "His ever expanding, peaceful government will never end. He will rule forever with fairness and justice from the throne of his ancestor David. The passionate commitment of the LORD Almighty will guarantee this!"

We can still have trouble seeing evidence of Jesus' reign today. That's because there is an already-but-not-yet quality to his kingdom. Jesus is already King, and he rules from heaven over every part of the cosmos that does his will. Everything and every being in the universe obey his words—everything, that is, except human beings on one tiny planet. Here alone he temporarily allows his will *not* to be done, except by his followers who choose to serve him. But a day is coming when that will change. The Bible promises that Jesus will return one day and take his rightful place on the throne of the earth. When he does, he will defeat all of God's enemies once and for all. On that day every knee will bow and every tongue will confess that Jesus Christ is Lord (see Philippians 2:10-11). No one knows when this will take place, but because God promised it, we know it will happen. This hope has sustained believers throughout the centuries as we struggle to remain faithful to our King in the midst of a world that fights violently to kick him off his throne (see Psalm 2). The question is not *if* Jesus will return to include our planet fully into his kingdom, but *when*.

QUESTIONS

When will Jesus come back, and what will happen when he does?

As Jesus ascended into heaven forty days after he rose from the dead, his disciples stood staring into the sky watching him go. Most thought he would establish his kingdom on earth immediately, so his departure confused them. They strained to see him while they scrambled to figure out what his leaving meant. Suddenly two angels appeared and said, "Men of Galilee, why are you standing here staring at the sky? Jesus has been taken away from you into heaven. And someday, just as you saw him go, he will return!" (Acts 1:11).

Those who heard these words fully expected to witness his return in their lifetimes. They thought his second coming would be no more than a few short years away. So confident were they that the time was short that no one thought to write down all Jesus said and did until nearly twenty years after his ascension. For two thousand years believers have clung to the promise that Jesus will return, and every generation has believed it would be the one to see the promise come true.

Skeptics see the delay as proof that Jesus wasn't real to begin with, but believers know better. Peter explained the reason for Christ's delay: "The Lord isn't really being slow about his promise to return, as some people think. No, he is being patient for your sake. He does not want anyone to perish, so he is giving more time for everyone to repent" (2 Peter 3:9).

The promise of Jesus' second coming is the blessed hope that pulls us through difficult days and reassures us that one day we will see him face-to-face. He will then dispense long-delayed justice. The last traces of evil will be removed, and the

Devil, the old enemy who has made our lives miserable for so long, will be locked away once and for all. The last few chapters of the Bible tell us that God will then bring about a new heaven and a new earth that will so far outshine the old that our minds cannot comprehend what they will be like. But the sweetest part of the eternal age Jesus' second coming will usher in will be the unbroken intimacy we will share with our God. Revelation 7:17 promises, "For the Lamb who stands in front of the throne will be their Shepherd. He will lead them to the springs of life-giving water. And God will wipe away all their tears." That's what we are looking forward to in his second coming. This is the hope that drives us.

However, once we start discussing the whens and whos and hows of the Second Coming, things get confusing. Eschatology, the study of last things, has produced a wide variety of views with a unique vocabulary to describe what will happen. Believers all agree that Jesus will return. It's the details we don't see eye to eye on.

Key Passages

The hope of Jesus' return runs through the entire Bible. The Old Testament prophets spoke of the peace and prosperity the Messiah would usher in. Many scholars believe major portions of Daniel and Ezekiel describe the events surrounding Jesus' return and a future judgment of the entire world. These chapters include Daniel 7–12 and Ezekiel 38–48. In addition, God promises to create a new heaven and earth where "the wolf and lamb will feed together. The lion will eat straw like the ox. Poisonous snakes will strike no more. In those days, no one will be hurt or destroyed on my holy mountain. I, the LORD, have spoken!" (Isaiah 65:25).

In the New Testament, the major passages that give details of Jesus' return include Matthew 24–25 (and the parallel passages in Mark 13:1-31 and Luke 21:5-36), 1 Corinthians 15, 1 Thessalonians 4:13-18, 2 Thessalonians 2, 2 Peter 3, and the book of Revelation. This list isn't meant to be exhaustive. These are merely the passages to which those who write on eschatology most often refer. Matthew 24–25 is especially important, for it contains Jesus' response to the question, "Will there be any signs ahead of time to signal your return and the end of the world?"

The book of Revelation is the most exhaustive treatment of Jesus' second coming, as well as one of the hardest books in the Bible to understand. John, the writer, included a great deal of symbolic language that has been interpreted in many different ways over the past two thousand years. For example, he referred to the "whore of Babylon" in chapters 17–18. Some see this as a reference to Rome during John's time; others believe it refers to Babylon itself, which was located in modern Iraq. Still others equate it with everything from a revived Roman Empire to the Catholic Church to the United States of America.

A New Millennium

The last four chapters of Revelation describe the actual Second Coming and the ushering in of the eternal age. Within this description we find one of the key elements of eschatology: Christ's thousand-year reign, most often referred to as the millennial reign. Revelation 20:1-10 tells us that when Jesus returns, Satan will be captured and bound for a thousand years. At the same time, those who lost their lives for the sake of Jesus will rise from the dead and reign with Christ. After these thousand years have passed, the Devil will be set free for a short time. He will immediately gather the nations of the world together and lead them in a final rebellion against God. Fire from heaven will consume the enemy armies, and Satan will be thrown into the lake of fire for eternity.

Scholars differ on whether these events in Revelation 20 are to be taken literally or figuratively. The answers bring us to the first major dividing point between the divergent views of the Second Coming. *Postmillennialists* (literally "after the millennium") believe Jesus' reign will come through the spread and triumph of the gospel on earth. This view was especially popular during the Victorian period with its Enlightenment belief in progress. When the horrors of World War I replaced optimism with pessimism, postmillennialism waned.

The latter half of the twentieth century saw a new form of postmillennialism emerge that says God calls believers to take dominion over this earth. Also known as Christian Reconstructionism, this movement teaches that the gospel will triumph, permitting society to be reshaped according to biblical law. Then, after God's kingdom is established through the church, Christ will return as King. After he returns he will judge everyone according to what he or she has done. At that time the dead in Christ will be raised and all believers will be given eternal bodies. While some postmillennialists take the thousand years of Revelation 20 literally, most take it metaphorically to mean a very long time. Many also believe this millennial reign has already begun through the work of God's people, the church.

Amillennialism (that is, "no millennium," or, no literal thousand-year period) takes Revelation 20:1-10 figuratively, as a description of Christ's triumph and the reign of believers with him in heaven. According to this view, good and evil will coexist on earth until the day Jesus returns. On that day, the dead will be raised and judged for everything they have done. Believers will receive resurrection bodies that will last forever. Christ will not literally reign on earth for one thousand years before the Final Judgment. His kingdom exists already in the lives of believers. When he returns he will usher in his eternal kingdom, along with the new heaven and new earth. Amillennialists take the thousand years of Revelation 20 figuratively.

Many postmillennialists and amillennialists are also *preterists* —that is, they believe many if not all of the eschatological events in the Bible have already take place. The opposite of preterism is *futurism*, which says passages such as Matthew 24 and the book of Revelation describe events that will take place in the future. Preterists point to the destruction of Jerusalem by the Roman armies in AD 70 as the moment when these predictions came true. Full preterists, a minority view, go so far as to say Jesus returned in AD 70. They believe every eschatological event has already take place, including the resurrection of the dead and the Day of Judgment. Partial preterists believe that many, but not all, of the Bible's predictions regarding the Second Coming were fulfilled during the first century. But they see Jesus' return and the Final Judgment as future events.

The third major millennial view is called *premillennialism* (literally "before the millennium"). Premillennialists believe Christ will return before a literal thousand-year reign. They interpret Revelation 20:1-10 literally. All of the events contained in these verses will happen just as they are written, in the order in which they are written, at some point in the future. Whereas postmillennialists see Christ's reign coming gradually, premillennialists believe Christ's return will be a cataclysmic event accompanied by a period of global upheaval and suffering like the world has never known. This period of suffering is known as the *Great Tribulation* (see Revelation 7:14). During this time of tribulation, Satan will mobilize his forces and try to stamp out God's reign on earth. He will raise up the *Antichrist*, who will deceive the world with false miracles. The world will hail him as both a political leader and a god. Revelation 13 describes how only those who pledge their allegiance to the Antichrist, also known as the *Beast*, will be allowed to buy and sell and lead a normal life. Those who don't will be persecuted.

Premillennialists believe that when Jesus returns he will lay waste to the Antichrist and defeat Satan and his armies. Then Jesus himself will reign on earth for one thousand years. During the millennial kingdom, we will see how life could have been if sin had never entered the picture.

We Will All Be Changed

First Corinthians 15:51-55 brings the promise of Christ's return down to a very personal level. When Jesus returns, he will give his followers new bodies. Our current fragile bodies cannot inherit the kingdom that God has in store for us. Paul wrote:

> But let me tell you something wonderful, a mystery I'll probably never fully understand. We're not all going to die—*but* we are all going to be changed. You hear a blast to end all blasts from a trumpet, and in the time that you look up and blink your eyes—it's over. On signal from that trumpet from heaven, the dead will be up and out of their graves, beyond the reach of death, never to die again. At the same moment and in the same way, we'll all be changed. In the resurrection scheme of things, this has to happen: everything perishable taken off the shelves and

replaced by the imperishable, this mortal replaced by the immortal. Then the saying will come true:

> Death swallowed by triumphant Life!
> Who got the last word, oh, Death?
> Oh, Death, who's afraid of you now? (MSG)

This event is referred to as the *Rapture.* The word itself does not appear in the Bible. It comes from the Latin word *rapio,* which means caught up. The idea is taken from the passage above and 1 Thessalonians 4:13-18, which describes how we will be "caught up" in the clouds to greet Jesus as he returns. The Rapture includes the resurrection of those who died in Christ, as well as the transformation of the believers who are alive when Jesus returns. All of the millennial views believe this raising and changing will take place, although the term *Rapture* is usually associated with premillennialists.

Three Premillennialist Views

Among premillennialists, there are several views on the Rapture and its relationship to the tribulation period that premillennialists believe will accompany the Second Coming. *Pretribulationalists* believe Christ will return to rapture his church just before the Great Tribulation breaks out. This position points to Revelation 3:10 as God's promise to protect his children from this time of universal suffering. The pretribulational position is most often associated with *dispensational premillennialism.*

Dispensationalists believe God has worked in the world in different ways during different ages, or dispensations. The bulk of the Old Testament describes the age of Law, while the New

Testament describes the church age. In the age of Law, God dealt primarily with Israel. Since Christ's resurrection, God has dealt with the church. Dispensationalists believe the church age will end when the Tribulation begins. At that moment, Christ will remove his church from earth. According to this view, the Great Tribulation marks God's efforts once again to reach the Jews. Because of this, dispensationalists place a strong emphasis on events taking place in the Middle East today, and they stand up for the nation of Israel. After the seven years of tribulation (taken from Daniel 7, 9, and 12) Christ will return to the earth from heaven, bringing his resurrected and changed believers with him.

Posttribulationalists believe Christ will return only once, and that return will take place after the time of Tribulation. Posttribulationalists point out that the Bible never speaks of two second comings. Instead, Matthew 24:30-31 seems to indicate that God's angels will gather his children from across the earth as Jesus returns after the time of trouble has ended. The same is true of Revelation 18–19, where the bride of Christ, the church, is said to be ready for Christ's return at the end of the Tribulation. Posttribulationalists also point to Christians' repeated pleas to God in Revelation during the time of suffering at the end of time (see Revelation 6:10; 14:12) as evidence that believers will go through this time of trouble that will affect the entire earth. Some posttribulationalists are also dispensationalists, although many are *historical premillennialists*, so called because this view is found in the writings of many church leaders from the first three centuries, including Papias, Irenaeus, Justin Martyr, Tertullian, Hippolytus, Methodius, Commodianus, and Lactantius.

Finally, *midtribulationalists* believe the Rapture of the church will take place at the midpoint of the tribulation period. They base their belief on Daniel 7:25 and 12:7, both of which imply that the Antichrist will be given control over God's people for "time, times, and half a time," or three and a half years. Most premillennialists believe the entire Tribulation will last seven years, a timetable deduced from the seventy weeks of Daniel 9.

If all of this leaves you completely confused, you may well be a panmillennialist. It's not an official eschatological position. The term was coined to describe those who figure God will make everything pan out in the end.

Again, the most important truth running through all these positions is the fact that Jesus will return. When he does, all the whens and whys and whos will be settled once and for all.

section

4

The Holy Spirit

ESSENTIALS

God Up Close and Personal

Life in the Spirit

QUESTIONS

What is the baptism of the Holy Spirit?

Does the Spirit perform signs and wonders today?

For many believers, the Holy Spirit is the most mysterious and least understood member of the Trinity. God the Father we can grasp because we see examples around us of what fathers are supposed to be. Even those who grew up with no father or one who was, in the words of the band Death Cab for Cutie, little more than a donor of seed, can grasp the concept of fatherhood, even if it's simply the longing for a real dad. Jesus the Son is also easy for us to understand. We can see him in the pages of the Bible as he heals the sick and teaches us about the kingdom of God. Our hearts break when we read of his death on a cross. Even when we step away from the Bible, we see him. Messianic figures fill books and movies, from Aslan the Great Lion dying for Edmund in *The Lion, the Witch and the Wardrobe* to Neo giving his life to save Zion in *The Matrix* trilogy.

But we don't have a ready reference point for the Holy Spirit. His name evokes the mysterious and mystical. The King James Version translates his name as Holy Ghost, which makes him sound not only ethereal, but also frightening. Spirits and ghosts are the stuff of Halloween and scary movies—not exactly the things we associate with God. The one word believers most often associate with the Spirit is "power." Jesus told his disciples in Acts 1:8, "But when the Holy Spirit has come upon you, you will receive power." While the word describes part of what the Spirit does, it doesn't help us understand who he is. Power is something that comes out of the outlets on the living room wall. We usually think of it as an it, not a who.

Because of the mystery surrounding the Spirit, believers across the theological spectrum have widely varied views of him. Some groups associated with the Pentecostal and charismatic movements place a great deal of emphasis on the Spirit's activity in the world today. They believe the Spirit makes his presence known through signs and wonders, including miracles and speaking in tongues. Most mainline denominations, such as Methodists, Presbyterians, and Episcopalians, along with Baptists, shy away from tongues and other outward signs and wonders. That doesn't mean they don't believe in the work of the Holy Spirit. They do. But they differ on their ideas about how the Spirit works in the world today, even to the level of how and when Christians receive the Spirit.

So who is the Holy Spirit, the third member of the triune God? And how will understanding who he is and what he does change our lives? Exploring what the Bible teaches about the

Spirit is not optional, nor is it meant to be confusing. Jesus said the Holy Spirit would be a well of living water springing up within our souls (see John 7:38-39). May the Spirit wash over you and refresh you as you walk with Christ.

ESSENTIALS

God Up Close and Personal

God is everywhere. His presence fills the universe. Theologians refer to this as God's omnipresence. The psalmist used much simpler language. He simply asked,

> Is there anyplace I can go to avoid your Spirit?
>   to be out of your sight?
> If I climb to the sky, you're there!
>   If I go underground, you're there!
> If I flew on morning's wings
>   to the far western horizon,
> You'd find me in a minute—
>   you're already there waiting! (Psalm 139:7-10, MSG)

From the farthest reaches of the universe to the deepest trench in the ocean, God is there. When you live in his universe, you cannot escape him.

God may be everywhere, but there are times when he feels very far away. Job cried out in his pain,

> If I only knew where to find God, I would go to his throne and talk with him there. I would lay out my case and present my arguments. . . . I go east, but he is not there. I go west, but I cannot find him. I do not see him in the north, for he is hidden. I turn to the south, but I cannot find him. (Job 23:3-4,8-9)

Job isn't alone in feeling this way. God's omnipresence doesn't mean all people always feel his presence in a personal way. J. I. Packer defined omnipresence as "God's awareness of everything everywhere as he upholds it in its own being and activity."[1] This simply means God may be nearby, but that isn't the same as God relating to us intimately and personally.

That's why God sent his Spirit. When Jesus promised to send the Holy Spirit, he told his disciples,

> "I will ask the Father, and he will give you another Counselor, who will never leave you. He is the Holy Spirit, who leads into all truth. The world at large cannot receive him, because it isn't looking for him and doesn't recognize him. But you do, because he lives with you now and later will be in you. No, I will not abandon you as orphans—I will come to you." (John 14:16-18)

The Holy Spirit brings all the promises of God's presence down to us on a new level. Through him we experience the triune God up close and personal.

Presence

Seven weeks after Jesus ascended into heaven, God did something unlike he'd ever done in the history of the world. Jesus' followers were all gathered together when suddenly a rush of wind filled the room. Then everyone saw something that looked like flames settling on each of them. As if that wasn't enough of a shock, they all started talking in languages they'd never learned. The disciples rushed out of the room and into the crowded streets of Jerusalem, still speaking in languages they'd never learned. Hundreds of pilgrims from across the Roman Empire had come into the city for the Feast of Pentecost. These pilgrims understood the languages Jesus' disciples were speaking, and they heard the good news of Jesus for the first time. That day, more than three thousand people believed and were baptized as Jesus' followers.

The most radical aspect of that day wasn't the rushing wind or the flames. Nor was it the fact that one hundred or so of Jesus' followers spoke in languages they'd never studied before. This day marked a dramatic change in the way God worked with human beings. Prior to Pentecost, the Holy Spirit did not dwell permanently in believers. He came over people for a time, equipping them to do something extraordinary for God (such as Samson in Judges 14–16) or to speak for God (such as Saul in 1 Samuel 10:10). But God's Spirit did not live inside people. His presence filled the tabernacle and later the temple, but not people. Everything changed at Pentecost, when God's Spirit filled his followers.

This is who the Holy Spirit is. He is the member of the triune God who makes God's presence known in a personal way. Through him God doesn't just come near us. The Bible says the Holy Spirit takes up residence inside of us. Paul explained:

> But you are not controlled by your sinful nature. You are controlled by the Spirit if you have the Spirit of God *living in you*. (And remember that those who do not have the Spirit of Christ *living in them* are not Christians at all.) Since Christ *lives within you*, even though your body will die because of sin, your spirit is alive because you have been made right with God. The Spirit of God, who raised Jesus from the dead, *lives in you*. And just as he raised Christ from the dead, he will give life to your mortal body by this same Spirit *living within you*. (Romans 8:9-11, emphasis added)

According to Paul, the mark of a Christian is the presence of the Holy Spirit living inside of us. He isn't just there to watch the corpuscles shoot through our hearts. The Spirit draws us into fellowship with God through Christ. He lives within us to bring to fruition God's promise to "live in them and walk among them" (2 Corinthians 6:16). God wants to be our God, and he wants us to be his people. As the Spirit dwells in us, he lets us experience the depths of God's marvelous love (see Ephesians 3:17-19). He constantly reaffirms God's unending love for us. "For his Holy Spirit speaks to us deep in our hearts and tells us that we are God's children," Paul reassured his readers (Romans 8:16).

Before we move on, we need to stop and consider how radical this truth is. When the first man and woman sinned, they were driven from God's presence. As we've pointed out many times, sin cannot come into contact with a holy God. Even the heroes of the Old Testament had to interact with God from a distance. He appeared to Abraham and Moses and David and Solomon, and his Spirit came over many people at various times for different tasks, but God didn't live inside them as he now does through the Holy Spirit. But because Jesus removed everything that separated us from God when he died and rose again, we now enjoy an unbroken, unparalleled, personal, and intimate fellowship with God of which Old Testament believers could only dream. We will never experience a single moment of separation from God, for his Spirit lives inside us when we belong to Jesus. The disciples may have walked with Jesus for three years on this earth, but we now get to experience him on a much higher plane for as long as we live. How could anyone ever get used to something like this!

Helper

Jesus called the Holy Spirit the "Counselor" who will never leave us (see John 16:7). This is one passage where something truly is lost in translation. Jesus uses the word παρακλητος, which means counselor, but also so much more. The Amplified Bible uses seven words to translate the single Greek term: counselor, comforter, helper, advocate, intercessor, strengthener, and standby. So which is the best translation? All of the above. Together they describe who the Spirit is.

As counselor, he leads us into God's truth and gives us wisdom when we need it most (see John 16:13; James 1:5). He does this even before we come to Christ. Jesus said the Spirit would "convince the world of its sin, and of God's righteousness, and of the coming judgment" (John 16:8).

As comforter, he reassures us that nothing can separate us from God's love (see Romans 8:15-17,35-39). He shelters us from our fears and lets us feel God's mercy in a tangible way. We don't have to worry that he won't be there when we need him. Our God is a God of comfort who comforts us in *all* our troubles (see 2 Corinthians 1:3-7).

As helper, he fills us with God's power to do things for the Father that go far beyond our own abilities. We see the Spirit doing this in the book of Acts when Peter, who looked like such a coward at the end of the Gospels, suddenly emerged as a firebrand who wouldn't be quiet about Jesus.

As advocate, the Spirit pleads our case, like a lawyer pleading his client's case before a judge. That's what the Spirit does on our behalf before the Father.

As intercessor, the Spirit prays for us. Paul wrote,

And the Holy Spirit helps us in our distress. For we don't even know what we should pray for, nor how we should

> pray. But the Holy Spirit prays for us with groanings that cannot be expressed in words. And the Father who knows all hearts knows what the Spirit is saying, for the Spirit pleads for us believers in harmony with God's own will. (Romans 8:26-27)

When we cannot pray, he takes over.

As strengthener, he builds us up, allowing us to stand when we would rather run away. The Holy Spirit strengthened Stephen in this way in Acts 7. An angry mob rushed at him, stones in their hands, but Stephen didn't cower in fear. Filled with the Spirit, he looked up toward heaven to see Jesus standing by his throne. We may never face anything so perilous, but that doesn't matter. The Spirit gives us strength to take bold stands for God no matter how timid we may be otherwise.

And as standby, the Spirit is always at our side. We could say that side is the inside, because that is where he dwells. He makes good on God's promise, "'I will never fail you. I will never forsake you.' That is why we can say with confidence, 'The Lord is my helper, so I will not be afraid. What can mere mortals do to me?'" (Hebrews 13:5-6).

Reveling in Obscurity

In John 12:20-21, a group of Greeks approached Philip, one of the twelve disciples, and asked, "Sir, we want to see Jesus. Can you help us?" (MSG). Answering this question is what the Holy Spirit delights in doing. Jesus said of him, "But when he, the Spirit of truth, comes, he will guide you into all truth. He will not speak on his own; he will speak only what he hears, and he will tell you what is yet to come. He will bring glory to me by taking from what is mine and making it known to you" (John 16:13-14, NIV). The Spirit doesn't draw attention to himself. Rather, he glorifies Jesus. Before we can come to Christ, the Spirit first must open our eyes to our deep need for salvation and show us the wonder of the cross. Then, after we come to Christ, he glorifies Jesus by focusing our attention on him and awakening within us a desire to be more and more like Christ.

This is one of the reasons why many believers so easily overlook the Spirit's work. He does everything described above without drawing attention to himself. J. I. Packer compared the way the Spirit glorifies Jesus to a floodlight illuminating a building. "It is as if the Spirit stands behind us, throwing light over our shoulder, on Jesus, who stands facing us. The Spirit's message to us is never, 'Look at me; listen to me; come to me; get to know me,' but always, 'Look at *him*, and see his glory.'"[2] Packer went on to say that the Spirit acts like a matchmaker whose role is to bring us together with Jesus and make sure we stay together.

This role of the Holy Spirit doesn't just tell us who he is. It also reveals his essential character. Again, the Spirit isn't an impersonal force or in any way inferior to the Father or the Son. But, like Jesus in Philippians 2, he doesn't feel the need to assert his primacy. He happily takes on a servant's role, glorifying Jesus, who in turn glorifies his Father. We will take an in-depth look at the way the Spirit works in the next chapter. For now, however, we find that his character challenges us to examine the way we live. The God who tells us to humble ourselves before him shows us how to live this out through the daily, internal example of the Spirit in our lives.

Life in the Spirit

The day Samuel anointed Saul as the first king of Israel, he told him to go to Gibeah, where the Lord's prophets stayed. "At that time the Spirit of the LORD will come upon you with power, and you will prophesy with them," Samuel told him. "You will be changed into a different person" (1 Samuel 10:6). This verse is the best description of what happens when the Holy Spirit enters your life. When God's Spirit moves in, you will be changed into a different person. He guarantees it.

Remade in Jesus' Image

Salvation doesn't just give us a fresh start or a second chance. When we receive Christ, we receive a brand-new life. Jesus called it being born again or being born of the Spirit. When God takes away our sins through Christ and sends his Spirit into our lives, we become completely new people. "If anyone is in Christ, he is a new creation; the old has gone, the new has come!" Paul wrote in 2 Corinthians 5:17 (NIV). This is especially true of the way God views us. As we saw in the chapter on the cross, Jesus' death and resurrection make us completely innocent in God's eyes, as pure in his sight as if we'd never sinned.

The Holy Spirit takes what is true of us in our standing before God and makes it a reality in our day-to-day lives. This process is known as sanctification. For the rest of our lives, he will be continually reshaping our thoughts, feelings, choices, and habits to bring them more and more in line with the way Jesus would think, feel, make decisions, and act if he had our circumstances and personality. The word that best describes the Spirit's goal is holiness. "You must be holy because I, the LORD, am holy. I have set you apart from all other people to be my very own," God told Israel (Leviticus 20:26). Peter said this remains God's goal for his children: "Obey God because you are his children. Don't slip back into your old ways of doing evil; you didn't know any better then. But now you must be holy in everything you do, just as God—who chose you to be his children—is holy. For he himself has said, 'You must be holy because I am holy'" (1 Peter 1:14-16).

The word *holy* means to be different, set apart, other. Holiness is more than simply avoiding sin, although that's a key element of it. True holiness causes our lives to stand out as different as our characters and passion look more like Jesus and less like our old ways of life. The Spirit brings this about as he sets us apart for God and sets us free from our old confused thinking and selfish habits. If we cooperate with him in this work, we will be visibly different from those who don't know God—not just because we don't do this and don't do that, but because we *do* the things God wants done in the world.

As the Spirit remakes our minds and wills, we are like trees bearing fruit. Paul explained, "But when the Holy Spirit controls our lives, he will produce this kind of fruit in us: love, joy, peace, patience, kindness, goodness, faithfulness, gentleness, and self-control" (Galatians 5:22-23). This is more than a list of character qualities God would like to see in us. This description appears in the midst of one of the sharpest warnings against legalism in the New Testament. Depending on the Law—that is, trying to keep a list of rules to make ourselves acceptable to God—will always end in frustration, Paul told the Galatians. Instead, we are to live by the Spirit through faith (see Galatians 5:5). As we yield ourselves to the Spirit's control, he changes us so that we become habitually loving, joyful, peaceful, patient, and so on.

There is disagreement within the Christian family as to how quickly this change takes place. John Wesley, founder of the Methodist movement of the eighteenth century, which in turn birthed the holiness movement, taught that sanctification could be attained instantly by faith. Although he did not equate this with instantaneous sinless perfection, Wesley saw sanctification as not merely a process, but a promise we can receive from God just as we receive salvation.[3] Wesley also taught that the sanctifying work of the Spirit can lead the believer to a place where he or she will no longer sin. This is also known as Christian perfectionism, a doctrine held by many holiness and Wesleyan denominations.

Other scholars understand sanctification to be a gradual process rather than an all-at-once experience. Millard Erickson called it a progressive matter that continues on throughout the believer's life.[4] Those who see sanctification as a process cite Philippians 1:6: "And I am sure that God, who began the good work within you, will continue his work until it is finally finished on that day when Christ Jesus comes back again." This verse also seems to indicate that this work will never reach a point of absolute perfection until the day Christ returns. Sinless perfection is thus unreachable until the last traces of sin are removed at the Second Coming.

Most Christian traditions recognize practices we can do to cooperate with the Spirit's work of sanctification. Wesley encouraged people to meet together in groups to pray, learn the Scriptures, and publicly confess their sins. Other traditions urge habits such as worship, service, prayer, and fasting. There is general agreement that we can't simply sit in front of the TV and expect the Spirit to change us effortlessly, yet the difference between effort and legalism remains an ongoing discussion.

Gifts of the Spirit

In addition to producing godly character, the Holy Spirit also equips us to serve God in unique ways. He does this by giving us spiritual gifts, or special abilities. These gifts are to be used for the benefit of the entire Christian family, the church (see 1 Corinthians 12:7). We will explore what the church is and its role in Christians' lives in a later chapter. Yet as we examine the ways the Spirit works in our individual lives, we need to remember that his work has a corporate element. This is especially true of the special abilities he gives us. He doesn't give them for our personal use. We're to use them to glorify God by building up other people.

The New Testament gives three lists of the special abilities the Spirit imparts:

- Prophesying, serving others, teaching, encouraging others, generosity, leadership, and showing kindness (see Romans 12:6-8)

- The ability to give wise advice, the gift of special knowledge, faith, the power to heal the sick, the power to perform miracles, prophecy, the ability to discern whether it is really the Spirit of God speaking or another spirit, the ability to speak in unknown languages, the ability to interpret what is being said in the unknown languages, and the ability to get others to work together (see 1 Corinthians 12:8-11, 28)

- Speaking and helping others (see 1 Peter 4:10-11)

In addition, Ephesians 4:11-13 lists leadership positions that are also gifts from God's Spirit to the entire church:

- Apostles
- Prophets
- Evangelists
- Pastors
- Teachers

The wide assortment of gifts shows the variety of ways God works through people to further his kingdom. Scholars disagree as to whether these lists should be thought of as exhaustive. For example, computers and digital video equipment obviously didn't exist two thousand years ago. Some would say it's possible that the ability to use these tools in a way that draws people closer to the Lord through worship or evangelism is a spiritual gift. In fact, one may well say that the Holy Spirit will give someone the ability to fulfill every need the church faces.

It's also worthwhile to note that not all gifts are equally visible. Some, such as the ability to speak unknown languages and the ability to perform miracles, appear very dramatic and exciting, while serving others and showing kindness can go completely unnoticed. However, according to the New Testament, all of the gifts are equally important to the overall work of God's kingdom. For the church to function properly and reach its full potential, every believer needs to use his or her Spirit-given abilities.

The Giver, not the receiver, chooses who receives what. Paul wrote, "It is the one and only Holy Spirit who distributes these gifts. *He alone decides which gift each person should have*" (1 Corinthians 12:11, emphasis added). We don't decide which gift we should have. That's the Holy Spirit's decision. When he enters our lives, he equips us to serve God in a unique way. Using his gift may make us very visible to other believers or unbelievers, or we may have to stay in the shadows. Either way, the point is doing whatever God has planned for our lives. Spiritual gifts allow us to live out the truth of Ephesians 2:10: "For we are God's masterpiece. He has created us anew in Christ Jesus, so that we can do the good things he planned for us long ago."

QUESTIONS

What is the baptism of the Holy Spirit?

When asked if he was the Messiah, John the Baptist didn't just say no. He went on to say, "I baptize with water; but someone is coming soon who is greater than I am—so much greater that I am not even worthy to be his slave. He will baptize you with the Holy Spirit and with fire" (Luke 3:16). The Someone he was talking about was, of course, Jesus. Right before Jesus ascended into heaven, he promised, "John baptized with water, but in just a few days you will be baptized with the Holy Spirit" (Acts 1:5). It didn't take long for his words to come true. Ten days later the Holy Spirit fell on the disciples on the day of Pentecost (see Acts 2).

What exactly happened when the Spirit came upon the disciples? And is their experience of being baptized by the Holy Spirit something every believer should experience? The New Testament actually contains very few references to the baptism of the Spirit. Of these, only one is unconnected to John the Baptist's description of Jesus or Jesus' promise in Acts 1:5. This one reference is found in 1 Corinthians 12:13: "Some of us are Jews, some are Gentiles, some are slaves, and some are free. But we have all been baptized into Christ's body by one Spirit, and we have all received the same Spirit."

The New Testament may not use the phrase "baptized in the Spirit" very often, but believers do today. The question of what being baptized in the Spirit means and how it takes place marks a major dividing line in the Christian family. Charismatic and Pentecostal believers teach that the baptism of the Holy Spirit is a separate event from salvation. They also teach that people will speak in unknown languages or tongues when they receive the

Spirit.[5] For these groups, tongues are necessary to confirm the Spirit's presence in each believer's life. By contrast, Christians outside charismatic and Pentecostal circles believe we receive the Holy Spirit when we enter God's family by faith. Many reject the idea that tongues as found in the book of Acts still exist today, and others believe they exist but aren't essential for every believer. Yet for Pentecostals, the baptism of the Spirit and speaking in tongues form a major part of their theological identity. How can these two groups reach such different conclusions?

The Baptism

The word *baptism* comes from the Greek word $\beta\alpha\pi\tau\iota\zeta\omega$, which means to dip or to wash. It was used to describe the sinking of ships and the immersion of a piece of cloth into a vat of dye. When John the Baptist and Jesus used the word in relation to the Holy Spirit, they said believers would be baptized "$\varepsilon\nu$" the Spirit. This small Greek preposition is important. It describes locations, as well as the means by which something is done. It could be translated "in," "with," or "by." That means the Holy Spirit could be the thing into which we are baptized, or he may be the One doing the baptizing as we are immersed by him.

Believers on both sides of the Pentecostal/non-Pentecostal divide all agree that the Holy Spirit resides inside believers. However, when it comes to the phrase "baptism of the Holy Spirit" after Pentecost, many non-Pentecostals, using 1 Corinthians 12:13 as their point of reference, emphasize the Spirit as the One who baptizes us into the larger body of the family of Christ. The late Baptist theologian W. A. Criswell wrote: "When you were converted, when you were regenerated, when you were saved, you became a Christian, the Holy Spirit took you and joined you to the body of Christ. He baptized you into the body of our Lord."[6] At the same moment the Spirit baptizes us into the body of our Lord—that is, the family of God consisting of all believers across time and space—he also takes up residence inside of us. Francis Schaeffer summed up this idea succinctly: "When we are justified, we are also immediately indwelt by the Holy Spirit."[7]

How, then, do theologians of this stripe explain the fact that the Spirit's coming appears to be separate from salvation in the book of Acts? This is true not only in Acts 2, but also in Acts 8, where the Samaritans received the Spirit after the apostles laid hands on them; Acts 9, where Paul received the Spirit when he was baptized; and Acts 19, where believers in Ephesus received the Spirit after Paul laid hands on them and prayed for the Spirit to come. In addition, the first Gentile believers to receive the Spirit did so at the moment they were saved. But, as on Pentecost, these Gentiles began speaking in tongues when the Spirit came upon them. Charismatics and Pentecostals point to these passages as proof that the baptism of the Holy Spirit is a separate experience that is accompanied by speaking in unknown languages.

Millard Erickson summarized the opposite position: "We note first that the Book of Acts speaks of a special work of the Spirit subsequent to a new birth. It appears, however, that the Book of Acts covers a transitional period. Since that time the normal pattern has been for conversion/regeneration and the baptism of the Holy Spirit to coincide."[8] Erickson and others find support for this view in other statements within the New Testament, including 1 Corinthians 12:13, which says we have all been baptized into Christ's body by one Spirit. How could this be true if some believers have not yet received the Spirit? The same can be said of Romans 8:9, which states, "Those who do not have the Spirit of Christ living in them are not Christians at all." If you must possess the Spirit to be a Christian, God must pour out his Spirit on all believers the moment they say yes to him. In the same way, if the baptism is a separate, vital experience, why doesn't the Bible command us to be baptized in or by the Holy Spirit? This argument of silence is one more proof for many believers that God pours out his Spirit on us at the moment of salvation.

Pentecostals agree that the Spirit enters all believers at the moment of conversion. However, they say that this experience, though precious, does not exhaust God's supply of what is available to all Christians. They point to the constant hunger for more of God that beats within us as proof that God has another, life-changing experience waiting for us. How can this be if the Spirit already dwells inside of us? Many say there is a difference between the Spirit being *with* you, and the Spirit being *in* you. The latter implies a greater level of control that the Spirit takes in our lives when we are baptized into him. Pentecostals would therefore agree that at conversion, the Spirit baptizes us into the body of Christ. However, they would say that being baptized εν the Spirit means being immersed or washed over and completely covered by the Holy Spirit of God.

The classic charismatic/Pentecostal position is summarized by a position paper from one of the largest Pentecostal groups in the world, the Assemblies of God church. It explains the baptism of the Spirit in the following:

> All believers are entitled to and should ardently expect and earnestly seek the promise of the Father, the baptism in the Holy Ghost and fire, according to the command

of our Lord Jesus Christ. This was the normal experience of all in the early Christian church. With it comes the enduement of power for life and service, the bestowment of the gifts and their uses in the work of the ministry (Luke 24:49; Acts 1:4,8; 1 Corinthians 12:1-31). This experience is distinct from and subsequent to the experience of the new birth (Acts 8:12-17; 10:44-46; 11:14-16; 15:7-9). With the baptism in the Holy Ghost come such experiences as an overflowing fullness of the Spirit (John 7:37-39; Acts 4:8), a deepened reverence for God (Acts 2:43; Hebrews 12:28), an intensified consecration to Him and a dedication to His work (Acts 2:42), and a more active love for Christ, for His Word, and for the lost (Mark 16:20).[9]

Pointing to the book of Acts, they say the initial evidence of this event is speaking in tongues.[10]

The baptism of believers in the Holy Ghost is witnessed by the initial physical sign of speaking with other tongues as the Spirit of God gives them utterance (Acts 2:4). The speaking in tongues in this instance is the same in essence as the gift of tongues (1 Corinthians 12:4-10,28), but different in purpose and use.[11]

They say this is not an end in itself, but a means to an end. The baptism of the Spirit introduces believers to the ongoing process of living a Spirit-empowered life. At the moment of salvation, we experience the transforming work of the Spirit. Through the baptism, we enter into the empowering work of the Spirit, a work that is to continue throughout the rest of our lives.

Filled with the Spirit

While the Bible doesn't command us to be baptized in the Spirit, it does tell us to be filled by him. Ephesians 5:18 tells us, "Don't be drunk with wine, because that will ruin your life. Instead, let the Holy Spirit fill and control you." Placing these two commands next to one another helps us understand what it means to let the Holy Spirit fill and control us. When someone fills himself up with alcohol, the liquor takes over. The person loses control and acts completely different. There's no mistaking a drunk. They way he acts shows that the alcohol is making him act as he does.

The same is true of the Spirit filling and controlling our lives. The way this command is constructed in the original language implies we are to constantly seek to be filled with the Spirit. Essentially, we're to become Spirit-aholics. Every day we're to ask God to fill us with his Spirit and take complete control of our lives. In the Bible, when the Spirit took over, incredible things happened. He filled his children with power, boldness, confidence, wisdom, and passion for both God and other people that no person could ever muster on her own.

Both Pentecostals and non-Pentecostals agree that living a Spirit-filled life is vital. Even the staunchest, most non-tongue-speaking, anti-Pentecostal believer would agree that all of us need a deepened reverence for God, an intensified consecration to him and a dedication to his work, and a more active love for Christ, for his Word, and for the lost—the very things Pentecostals say occur when a person receives the baptism of the Spirit. However, non-Pentecostals point to these as the results of being continually filled with the Spirit.

Does this mean the two sides are saying basically the same thing? Not exactly. The question of tongues, along with signs and wonders, marks a line of demarcation between these two theological points of view. However, when believers from both sides of the aisle are filled with the Spirit, these differences should not prevent them from working together to further God's kingdom on earth. Since two of the fruits of the Spirit are love and peace, those who claim to have the Spirit dwelling inside them should show these qualities to one another in spite of their differences. Otherwise, all the talk of the Spirit is nothing but noise.

Does the Spirit perform signs and wonders today?

"The truth is, anyone who believes in me will do the same works I have done, and even greater works, because I am going to be with the Father. You can ask for anything in my name, and I will do it, because the work of the Son brings glory to the Father. Yes, ask anything in my name, and I will do it!" (John 14:12-14)

Jesus said this to encourage his disciples on their last night together. Over the next twenty-four hours, the disciples' world would fall apart. One of them would disappear, and they would soon learn that he had betrayed Jesus. Then a mob would arrest their Lord. As night gave way to day, they would watch as he was put on trial, mocked, beaten, and finally crucified.

Yet before any of that happened, Jesus wanted them to know that even though his work on earth was now done, they would pick up where he left off. The disciples wouldn't just do the things Jesus did. They would do greater things! When you consider a few of the miracles Jesus performed, his words set the imagination to flight. During his three-year ministry, he healed the sick, opened the eyes of the blind, made the lame walk, and raised the dead, to say nothing of walking on water and ordering storms around. In between, he drove out herds of demons from possessed people and fed more than nine thousand people with nothing more than a few loaves of bread and a handful of fish.[12] How could anyone top this? Yet that was exactly what Jesus told his disciples they would do.

This isn't the only place Jesus spoke of the miraculous feats his followers would accomplish in his name. In Mark 16:17-18, Jesus said,

> "These signs will accompany those who believe: They will cast out demons in my name, and they will speak new languages. They will be able to handle snakes with safety, and if they drink anything poisonous, it won't hurt them. They will be able to place their hands on the sick and heal them."

These verses are part of what is known as the longer ending of Mark. There are questions as to whether Mark actually wrote these words or if they were added later by someone making a handwritten copy of Mark that then went into circulation. The textual evidence points to the latter. However, according to the book of Acts, Jesus' followers did the very things mentioned in these verses. They cast out demons. They healed the sick. Paul escaped harm even when bitten by a poisonous snake. Peter didn't even have to lay hands on sick people to heal them. Just his shadow falling over them was enough. By the time you reach the end of the book of Acts, you see that Jesus' words came true.

Will they still come true today? Can believers in the twenty-first century expect to not only witness, but also perform, the kind of miraculous signs and wonders enjoyed by believers in the first century? Like the question of the baptism of the Holy Spirit, the answers to these questions generally come down to the divide between charismatic/Pentecostal believers and non-Pentecostals.

The Charismatic/Pentecostal Position

All believers agree that the Spirit still gives people the ability to fulfill vital roles in God's kingdom. However, no one ever gets in an argument over whether or not the Spirit still gives people the ability to encourage the brokenhearted. When people say they believe the gifts of the Spirit are still given today, they are usually talking about what are referred to as "sign gifts" — that is, the gifts that result in outward miracles, especially healing, as well as the gift of unknown languages or tongues.

Pentecostal believers assert that the pattern found in the book of Acts still holds today. Christians should still experience the fullness of the Spirit that the early church enjoyed. Therefore, we can expect the sick to be healed, the lame to walk, and the blind to see. The late John Wimber, one of the founders of the Vineyard Movement and author of *Power Healing* and *Power Evangelism*, reached this conclusion after reading the stories of miracles in the Bible and comparing them to the boring church services he attended as a new Christian. He finally asked a Bible study leader when they would get to do the stuff people did in the Bible, such as raising the dead and healing the sick. The expectation to be able to "do the stuff" permeates charismatic theology.

This "stuff" includes speaking in tongues, which, as we saw in the last chapter, Pentecostals believe is the initial evidence of receiving the baptism of the Holy Spirit. This position teaches that even those who do not possess the public gift of tongues mentioned in 1 Corinthians 12 will still experience tongues as a private prayer language to God. This they equate with the Holy Spirit praying for us with groanings too deep for words (see Romans 8:26-27).

In addition to this private prayer language, Pentecostals say, some people have the gift of speaking an unknown language (see 1 Corinthians 12:10), which they should use when the church is gathered together as long as an interpreter is present (see 1 Corinthians 14:27). The gift of tongues must be allowed, for Paul himself wrote, "I thank God that I speak in tongues more than all of you" (1 Corinthians 14:18) and later, "Don't forbid speaking in tongues" (1 Corinthians 14:39). This unknown language is not a human language such as French or German. Rather, charismatics and Pentecostals believe these tongues are the heavenly language or "tongues of angels" Paul referred to in 1 Corinthians 13:1 (NIV).

The "stuff" also includes divine healing. Most Pentecostal groups teach that not only will God heal the sick through the laying on of hands, but also that healing for God's children is guaranteed in Christ's atonement. The Assemblies of God church's position paper on healing states, "Atonement provides for the consequences of sin. Even where sickness is not the direct result of sin, it is still in the world because of sin. Therefore it is among the works of the Devil Jesus came to destroy (1 John 3:8) and is thus included in the atonement."[13] The same paper goes on to explain how healing is a privilege available to every believer. However, the Assemblies of God, as well as many other Pentecostal groups, make it clear that no one can demand healing from God. Nor does healing insulate us from the effects of aging and death. They also remind us that just because believers are guaranteed the privilege of divine healing doesn't mean they should never consult a doctor or take steps to assure both physical and mental health.

Not all Pentecostal groups make this distinction. An offshoot of the charismatic movement known as the Word of

Faith movement, or "positive confession," teaches that not only is healing available in the atonement, but God also must heal us when we ask. This line of teaching also places great emphasis on a believer's words, or confession. The movement teaches that you can avoid bad things in life by avoiding negative confession, and you will receive the best in life through making positive confession. Simply put, if you believe good thoughts and say good things, good stuff will happen to you. But if you think negative thoughts and whine and complain, bad things will happen to you. Included in most Word of Faith teachings is an emphasis on material prosperity. God wants to make every believer wealthy as well as healthy. Failure to achieve these ends lies not in God, but in the believer who doesn't exercise enough faith to receive all God wants to give.

Tongues and healing are not the only sign gifts Pentecostals believe the Holy Spirit pours out today. They confidently expect God to perform all kinds of signs and wonders, including not only tongues and healing, but also miracles, exorcisms, and prophetic words, just as he did two thousand years ago. After all, they say, God is the same yesterday, today, and forever (see Hebrews 13:8). Why should we expect anything different?

The Non-Pentecostal Position

Lumping every other group together can be dangerous, especially in response to a subject as broad as the signs and wonders the Holy Spirit may or may not perform today. However, because of space, we have no other choice. Keep in mind that the following is a very general summary.

Non-Pentecostals approach the question of the Spirit's signs and wonders in a different way. Some, such as pastor John MacArthur, teach that all signs and wonders ceased when the last of the apostles died. Why would God change the way he works like this? Those holding this view say God hasn't changed. Reading through the Bible as a whole, one finds that miracles were actually rare. God reserved them for particular moments in history when he revealed himself in an unmistakable way. Those who hold this view believe God answers prayer, including working in a way that defies natural explanations. However, they see this as very different from the miracles Jesus and the apostles performed.

In the Old Testament, almost all of the recorded miracles occurred during the lifetimes of Moses and the prophets Elijah and Elisha. God worked miracles through Moses to reveal himself to Israel as a nation as he called the people out of Egypt. These miracles were also God's stamp of approval on the Law. Elijah and Elisha spoke during a crucial moment in Israel's history as both the northern and southern kingdoms plunged deeper and deeper into idolatry.

The third era of miracles came in the New Testament through Jesus and the apostles. Many of Jesus' signs harkened back to what Moses and Elijah had done before him. Just in case we missed the connection, God reaffirmed it at the Transfiguration, when the two Old Testament heroes appeared on the mountain with Jesus (see Matthew 17:1-13; Mark 9:2-13; Luke 9:28-36). The signs Jesus performed confirmed his message and pointed to him as the Messiah who had come to save the world from sin. By extending these miracles to the apostles, Jesus confirmed his message once again and showed that the kingdom of God, which he inaugurated, had only just begun.

What does this have to do with miracles today? Everything. Since the Holy Spirit confirmed the gospel through signs and wonders at the hands of the apostles, the need for those signs has passed. The message stands as truth from God. This view points out that God never sent miracles to satisfy the curiosity of those who wanted to be amazed. Every miracle had a specific purpose: to confirm God's truth. Many believe God will send a fourth era of miracles at the very end of time through the two witnesses who will call the world to repentance during the tribulation period before the Lord's return (see Revelation 11).

At this point, two main schools of thought come to bear. One says that all miraculous signs have ceased throughout time and throughout the world. Since the gospel has been confirmed, the need for miracles has passed. The fact that miracles become more and more rare as you read through the book of Acts is evidence, in this view, that God meant the age of miracles to be temporary.

The other school of thought says that God will at times choose to send miraculous signs once again, but only rarely and only at great turning points when he makes himself known to a people. C. S. Lewis wrote, "God does not shake miracles into Nature at random as if from a pepper-caster. They come on great occasions: they are found at the great ganglions of history—not of political or social history, but of that spiritual history which cannot be fully known by men."[14]

One such instance was reported by Southern Baptist missionaries in the Shantung Province of China in the late 1920s and early 1930s. Generally speaking, Southern Baptists do not embrace Pentecostal theology. However, during the Shantung Revival, missionaries reported seeing miracles and healings, along with thousands of people coming to Jesus Christ for the very first time.[15] Other stories like this occasionally emerge from the mission field, although not all are verified.

As for the particular signs of tongues and healing, a similar response is given. Those who believe the baptism of the Holy Spirit comes at salvation do not believe tongues or any other outward signs are needed as initial evidence of receiving him. As for the gift of speaking in unknown languages spoken of in 1 Corinthians 12, some say that tongues have ceased. First Corinthians 13:8 says, "Prophecy and speaking in unknown languages and special knowledge will all disappear." Once God's Word was completed with the writing of the New Testament, the need for these gifts passed. No longer do we need prophets to speak for God. We can read his Word ourselves, this view maintains.

Not all non-Pentecostals believe tongues have ceased. However, most are skeptical that the ecstatic utterances found in the tongues of the charismatic movement are in fact the tongues of the New Testament. As evidence, they point to the fact that the tongues in Acts 2 were known languages that the disciples were able to speak without first learning them. It would be like a girl from Indiana suddenly speaking French even though everything she knew about the language came from watching Pepé Le Pew cartoons.

Regarding healing, those outside Pentecostal circles disagree with the teaching that Jesus' death and resurrection guarantee physical health for us in this life. The passage in question is Isaiah 53:5: "But he was wounded and crushed for our sins. He was beaten that we might have peace. He was whipped, and we were healed!" For non-Pentecostals, this passage speaks of healing from sin, not from diseases. If healing is guaranteed, why then do people still die, as death is the ultimate result of sin? This view points to the fact that many of the strongest proponents of faith healing have died from diseases from which they couldn't heal themselves. This, they say, is further proof that physical healing is not guaranteed in Christ's atonement. If it were, death by cancer would be an even greater tragedy — a failure of faith, not just a loss of life.

While proponents of this view believe that healing is not guaranteed through Jesus' work on the cross, they do believe that God can and sometimes does choose to heal people in response to prayer. James 5:14-15 instructs those who are sick to ask the elders of the church to anoint them with oil and pray over them. Does this mean everyone a church's elders pray over will be healed? Not necessarily. Yet, for the believer, physical healing is not required for victory over affliction. When God refused to remove Paul's "thorn in the flesh," he told Paul, "My gracious favor is all you need. My power works best in your weakness." To this Paul replied, "So now I am glad to boast about my weaknesses, so that the power of Christ may work through me" (2 Corinthians 12:9). Even death is a victory. As Paul wrote, we will one day take up the taunt, "O death, where is your victory? O death, where is your sting?" (1 Corinthians 15:55). This is the ultimate healing — the privilege of being absent from the body so we can be at home with the Lord (see 2 Corinthians 5:6-8).

5

Knowing God

ESSENTIALS

Made for More

By Grace Through Faith

Faith into Life

True Community

QUESTIONS

Can salvation be lost?

What's the deal with baptism?

How involved should believers be in the political process?

Does my gender limit what I can do for God?

What happens when people die?

Theology begins with the God who speaks. It expands our understanding of the triune God: Father, Son, and Holy Spirit. Yet it doesn't stop there. Theology doesn't just open our eyes to God. It opens our eyes to ourselves and enables us to understand who we are, why we act the way we do, and how we can reach our full potential and purpose as God's unique creations. Ideas shape our lives, and our views of ourselves determine much about how we live. We need more than positive self-images. Each of us needs to develop a biblical self-image—that is, an understanding of ourselves rooted in eternal truth.

The Bible has a lot to say about the human animal. For starters, it tells us we aren't just animals. Nor are we nameless, faceless cogs in the machine that is the universe. The Bible and Christian theology present the human race in a way that shows we have incredible worth, and that worth flows out of the God who made us in his image. He also created us for a reason. Theology tells us our lives matter. We have purpose for living. Life isn't just a long line of chance encounters and coincidences. God has a plan that we can discover and live out.

The Bible also sets us free to be fully human. We aren't prisoners of our circumstances and appetites. Christ died and rose again to make us much, much more. He came, the Bible tells us, that we might have life to the full (see John 10:10). That means we aren't really living until we're living in him. Then, and only then, are we set free to soar and reach the full potential God built in us when he formed us inside our mothers' wombs.

As we plunge into this area of our study of God, we find the only way to become fully human is through knowing God. Real life begins with him. Pastor Rick Warren said, "You were made by God and for God—and until you understand that, life will never make sense."[1] Yet this raises a question: If God made us to know him, why don't we know him automatically? That's where we will begin. God made us for himself, but something got in the way a long, long time ago.

ESSENTIALS

Made for More

As human beings, we were made to know God. If this is true, it would seem logical to assume that every person on the planet would enjoy a relationship with him. After all, God also made us to eat food, drink water, and breathe air. No matter where we go, from a billionaire's mansion to a tribal village in the middle of a rainforest, we will find people eating and drinking and breathing. It comes naturally. We were also made to love and be loved by other people. Relationships are a major part of what it means to be human, because that's how God designed us. No one has to tell a newborn baby to cry for its mother or to snuggle down and fall asleep in the loving arms of its father. We are born with an automatic desire to connect to other people.

But God is different. Many people go through life without ever giving him a thought, and they seem to manage just fine. While we would like to think that people who don't have a personal relationship with God are always miserable, lonely souls who desperately want to find something better, we know that isn't always the case. C. S. Lewis once said the happiest people he knew were often the most self-absorbed, nonreligious ones. If we are made to know God, how can this be?

And why would God seem so far away from us, if we were indeed made to know him? I know we just spent several chapters exploring the ways God reaches down to us through his Word, his Son, and his Spirit, but I want us to think through this question from a purely human point of view. We don't need a special book to tell us how to breathe. Nor do we need the stacks of books, songs, and movies on love to know what love is when it hits us.

Why doesn't knowing God work this way? I'm not saying the human heart doesn't long to know God. The longing is there. If we listen to our hearts, we can feel it. Every time a Super Bowl–winning quarterback goes on *60 Minutes* and wonders if there's something more to life, we witness the longing for God bubbling up to the surface. Yet people often don't realize that it's God for whom their hearts are aching. John Mayer didn't include God in his list of things he needed in his song "Something's Missing." Why don't we understand that the hunger in our souls is actually God calling us to him? And why can't anything else satisfy the hunger? Perhaps the bigger question is this: Why do some people go through their entire lives without feeling a longing for him at all?

The Bible offers a simple yet profound answer to these questions. It tells us we were indeed made to know God. He made us in his image to know and enjoy him. Yet along the way something came between us and God, something called sin. When sin entered the human heart, everything changed. Therefore, before we can explore what it means to know God, we need to understand the two key truths about the human race, two truths that open our eyes to how people can be so wonderful and so terrible at the same time.

In God's Image

According to the Bible, the human race was the last thing God made when he created the heavens and the earth. Unlike the rest of creation, he didn't just speak a word and cause people to spring into existence. Before he made the first man and woman, he said, "Let us make people in our image, to be like ourselves. They will be masters over all life—the fish in the sea, the birds in the sky, and all the livestock, wild animals, and small animals." Then the Bible says, "So God created people in his own image; God patterned them after himself; male and female he created them" (Genesis 1:26-27).

This is what sets you and me apart from everything else in the universe. Only people were made in God's image. He patterned us after himself. This means that we share several characteristics with God. Like him, we are creative. His image spills out when a hunk of Play-Doh in the hands of a preschooler becomes a horsey or a ducky. Humans like to create. Some people use words to invent stories, while others turn the rhythms in their heads into songs. Some draw pictures, while others draw plans that become bridges or buildings. You may not feel artistic, but that creative spark still comes out.

God's image in us is also what drives us to explore and understand the world. It's what prompts a guy to take things apart just to see how they work, even though he has no idea how to put them back together. Dogs don't send probes to the far reaches of space in a quest to learn more about how the universe was formed. Nor do monkeys devote their lives to exploring philosophical questions. But people do. We have a thirst for knowledge, an undying desire to understand the hows and the whys and the whats that surround us.

The image of God in us goes deeper than the things we do. God made us like himself so that we might reflect his glory. First Corinthians 11:7 calls us the image and *glory* of God. What does this mean? Simply this: God's image in us should reflect the character of God and, as a result, bring him glory. The best way to understand this is to think in terms of a football player who has the game of his life. Then, after the game, he hands the game ball to his dad. The boy played better than he ever has, but he wants the glory to go to his dad. That's the idea here. Because we are made in God's image, we reflect his glory whenever we put his image into practice. Not only that, but God also comes alongside us and empowers us whenever we act on his image. Whether we're drawing a picture or writing a song or planting a garden, whatever we do for the glory of God both brings him honor and draws us closer to him.

We can have this kind of relationship with God because he made us to be relational beings. The triune God, who has existed in an eternal relationship within himself through the Father, Son, and Holy Spirit, made us in such a way that our lives need to intertwine with the lives of others. We may feel as though our cocker spaniel loves us with an undying love, but any affection our pets may feel for us cannot compare to the love people experience with one another. And this love isn't optional. Paul said, "For the whole law can be summed up in this one command: 'Love your neighbor as yourself'" (Galatians 5:14). The Law isn't telling us anything we don't already know. The Beatles said all you need is love. Why? Because the God who is love made us in his image. He made us to love.

The heart of what it means to be made in God's image is that we're made to love him. Jesus said the first and greatest commandment is this: "Love the Lord your God with all your heart, all your soul, and all your mind" (Matthew 22:37). Before you jump to the conclusion that God shouldn't order us to love him, remember that God loved us first. John wrote, "We love because he first loved us" (1 John 4:19, NIV). By patterning humans after himself, God made us to relate to him, know him personally, and love him intimately. His image in us not only makes us self-aware; it makes us God-aware. Our hearts were made to long to love him.

Tainted by Sin

God made us to love him, but he refused to force himself on us. He created human beings with a choice. We can choose to love and obey him, or we can tell him to take a hike. The first man and woman were the only people to face this choice with perfect freedom, uncorrupted by sin in any way. When God made the first man and woman, he also planted a garden home for them. Somewhere in the garden, he planted a tree that he called the tree of the knowledge of good and evil. He told them, "You may freely eat any fruit in the garden except fruit from the tree of the knowledge of good and evil. If you eat of its fruit, you will surely die" (Genesis 2:16-17). The fruit on the tree wasn't poisonous, nor was the tree magical. Rather, it was a tangible way for the first man and woman to make a conscious choice to love and obey God. God's plan was for his special creation to resist temptation and learn what it meant to choose good and reject evil. Instead, the first man and woman embraced evil and rejected the good of freely obeying God.

Even though God warned them disobedience would mean death, Adam and Eve ate the forbidden fruit. Their perception of the world immediately changed. The Bible says, "At that moment, their eyes were opened, and they suddenly felt shame at their nakedness. So they strung fig leaves together around their hips to cover themselves" (Genesis 3:7). Not only did shame enter the world at that moment, but also guilt and excuse making. When God confronted the first couple, neither one would take responsibility for what he or she had done. The man blamed the woman, and the woman blamed the snake.

We might wonder what might have happened if they had both thrown themselves on the ground and begged for forgiveness. But of course, they didn't. Perhaps they didn't understand what a big deal this seemingly small act really was. People still struggle with this part of the story. Why was eating a piece of fruit so bad? But the fruit wasn't the point. Obeying God was. The first man and woman faced a choice: to humble themselves before God and take their place as creatures before their Creator, or to usurp God's authority and try to become gods themselves. They chose the latter, and their offspring continue to choose the same. This sin goes deeper than doing bad things as opposed to good things. A person can be the greatest guy in history and do more good works than Mother Teresa, but if he lives his life telling God he doesn't need him, or even worse, ignoring God as if he doesn't exist, none of the good matters. As Jesus showed in his interaction with the Pharisees, self-righteousness is the ugliest sin of all.

The first act of disobedience let loose every other act of disobedience. It was *the* turning point of human history. Theologians call the episode in the garden the Fall. Since that day, humans have shown there is no limit to how far the Fall will take us. If not for that first act of disobedience, the headlines wouldn't be filled with stories of wars and murders and abused children. Everything that makes life on earth unbearable, all of the cruelty people show toward one another — all of it has its roots in this first act of sin.

Sin not only corrupted the human race; it separated us from God. The first man and woman were driven from his presence, and the gulf remains to this day. Since the moment sin entered the world, God has seemed distant, if not absent. It's more than a physical distance. We feel a chasm between us, and it affects every person. Paul explained, "For all have sinned; all fall short of God's glorious standard" (Romans 3:23). In our natural state, before we come to God through Christ, we are dead in our sins (see Ephesians 2:1-3). In terms of a living connection with God, we don't have a pulse. Our hearts are cold toward him and as unaware of his presence as a corpse.

These two extremes of human nature show us how we can soar to such heights and sink to such depths, often within days. Made like God, we can create masterpieces. Corrupted by sin, those masterpieces can be lewd and offensive. The image of God in us moves us to love; the presence of sin causes us to hate. Yet more than that, these two extremes show the dilemma in which every person finds herself. We were made to know God, but we are separated from him by our sin. The depth of our sin is so great that we cannot save ourselves (see Ephesians 2:8-9). There is nothing we can do in our own effort to remove the stain sin leaves. Yet God's love is so great that he provided a way for those he made in his image, those he made to love him and know him, to be brought home. That is why Jesus did what we explored earlier.

Our sin shows us why we need salvation. God's image within us makes it possible. How then can we receive what God offers through Jesus' sacrifice on the cross?

By Grace Through Faith

It wasn't so long ago that you were mired in that old stagnant life of sin. You let the world, which doesn't know the first thing about living, tell you how to live. You filled your lungs with polluted unbelief, and then exhaled disobedience. We all did it, all of us doing what we felt like doing, when we felt like doing it, all of us in the same boat. It's a wonder God didn't lose his temper and do away with the whole lot of us. Instead, immense in mercy and with an incredible love, he embraced us. He took our sin-dead lives and made us alive in Christ. He did all this on his own, with no help from us! Then he picked us up and set us down in highest heaven in company with Jesus, our Messiah.

Now God has us where he wants us, with all the time in this world and the next to shower grace and kindness upon us in Christ Jesus. Saving is all his idea, and all his work. All we do is trust him enough to let him do it. It's God's gift from start to finish! We don't play the major role. If we did, we'd probably go around bragging that we'd done the whole thing! No, we neither make nor save ourselves. God does both the making and saving. He creates each of us by Christ Jesus to join him in the work he does, the good work he has gotten ready for us to do, work we had better be doing. (Ephesians 2:1-10, MSG)

In this passage, Paul explained how God solves the problem of our sin. Without Jesus, we were mired in an old stagnant life of disobedience and unbelief. The Fall made sure of that. Every human is in the same boat. The psalmist observed:

The LORD looks down from heaven
    on the entire human race;
he looks to see if there is even one with real
    understanding,
    one who seeks for God.
But no, all have turned away from God;
    all have become corrupt.
No one does good,
    not even one! (Psalm 14:2-3)

That's why saving us is all God's idea and all his work. As Ephesians 2:1-10 makes clear, there's nothing we can add to it. This idea sets Christianity apart from the world's other religions. This is not a religion of works, but of God's grace. People don't earn their way to heaven by doing more good things than bad. None of us can earn points with God by taking the trash out without being asked or doing random acts of kindness. According to the Bible, the only way we can be saved, the only way what Jesus did can affect our lives, is for us to trust God enough to let him do the saving. The Bible calls this faith, and it's impossible to please God without it (see Hebrews 11:6).

What Is Faith?

The Greek word usually translated faith, πιστις, is used 243 times in the New Testament. The verb form of the word, πιστευω, which means believe, is used 241 times, while the word for faithful, πιστος, appears another 67 times. The words appear so often because faith is central to our relationship with God. This has always been the case. When Paul defended the idea that we are made right with God by faith alone, he pointed to the Old Testament character

Abraham, who "believed the LORD, and the LORD declared him righteous because of his faith" (Genesis 15:6). You could even say the theme verse of the New Testament comes from the Old. Habakkuk 2:4 says, "The righteous will live by their faith." Habakkuk's words appear in Romans 1:17, Galatians 3:11, and Hebrews 10:38.

At the simplest level, the words *faith* and *believe* mean to think something is true. If you read a story in the paper that says the junior United States senator from your state is planning to run for president, you either believe the story is true or you don't. This is belief at its most basic level. However, biblical faith doesn't stop there. The words above mean believing in something to the extent that you trust in it completely. Your belief prompts you to act. You don't just believe your state's junior senator is going to make a run for the White House; you believe *in* his candidacy. You support him and tell all your friends to vote for him. When you explore the lives of biblical believers, you discover that the faith that pleases God not only believes he is real, not only believes he's wonderful, but also actively joins his side. This is the equivalent of believing so strongly in your state's junior senator that you volunteer to work in his campaign. Every day you stuff envelopes and work the phones and do anything else necessary to help make him the next president of the United States. This is what it means to believe.

Putting your faith in God requires an even more radical step. As the verses from the Bible that opened this chapter point out, before God saved us, we were actively working for the other side. We "used to live just like the rest of the world, full of sin, obeying Satan, the mighty prince of the power of the air" (Ephesians 2:2). Therefore, before we can turn to God in faith, we have to turn away from our old allegiance to Satan and our sinful desires. The Bible calls this repentance, and it is part of belief.

Jesus himself preached repentance. He told people, "The time has come. . . . The kingdom of God is near. Repent and believe the good news!" (Mark 1:15, NIV). Paul summarized the message he carried across the Roman Empire when he said, "I have had one message for Jews and Gentiles alike — the necessity of turning from sin and turning to God, and of faith in our Lord Jesus" (Acts 20:21). Turning from sin and turning to God are not two separate steps. Instead, the two phrases describe two parts of one act. Think of it this way: The act of voting for your favorite candidate is also a decision not to vote for the other guy. You cannot have one without the other.

The Basis of Faith

Faith works because it's based on something solid and true: God's Word. Paul said, "Faith comes from listening to this message of good news — the Good News about Christ" (Romans 10:17). The Message translation is even blunter: "The point is: Before you trust, you have to listen. But unless Christ's Word is preached, there's nothing to listen to." Biblical faith isn't just a shot in the dark, a mystical hope that God is out there somewhere. We sometimes use the word *believe* in this way. Every spring millions of Cubs fans say they believe this will be the year that their team finally wins the World Series, and they've been saying it every year since the Cubs' last title in 1908.

The hope that springs eternal during baseball's spring training isn't based on anything more than a wish and a prayer. That is not the case of biblical faith. Theology begins with the statement that God is and he has spoken, and this is where faith begins as well. We believe *because* God has spoken and acted. Our knowledge of the latter is inseparably linked to the former. We know what God did through ancient times and through his Son because the Bible tells us. While other historical records may back up some of the details, the Bible is our primary source of information about God. It is, therefore, the basis of our faith.

Faith starts with believing in the Bible as truth. It then moves to believe and trust in the specifics found within the Bible. This doesn't mean that as Christians we worship the Book rather than God. Our faith is in God, but we need to be clear that this God is the God of the Bible. He has revealed himself to us through it, and we enter into a relationship with him by believing and acting on what he has said.

The Object of Our Faith

In Acts 16, we find Paul and Silas locked away in a prison in the middle of the night. Rather than whine and complain, they sang praise songs to God. Suddenly, an earthquake hit and shook the cell doors open. The quake also woke the prison guard, who assumed all of the prisoners had fled. Because the penalty for letting prisoners escape was death, the guard drew his sword to take his own life. Paul stopped him and reassured him that everyone was present. The event so moved the guard that he fell down in front of Paul and Silas and asked, "Sirs, what must I do to be saved?" They replied, "Believe on the Lord Jesus and you will be saved, along with your entire household" (Acts 16:30-31). They shared the news of Jesus with him, and the man and all his family believed and were baptized.

Paul's message to the prison guard is the message of the New Testament. Yes, we are saved by faith. But that faith, that belief, has to be put in the right place. Simply believing there is a God is not enough. James 2:19 warns, "Do you still think it's enough just to believe that there is one God? Well, even the demons believe this, and they tremble in terror!" Faith that saves must be faith in Jesus Christ. Peter declared of Jesus, "There is salvation in no one else! There is no other name in all of heaven for people to call on to save them" (Acts 4:12).

Believing in Jesus means more than believing a guy named Jesus lived in Palestine in the first century. It even means more than acknowledging he had some good things to say. Faith in Jesus means believing all of what the Bible says about him, especially that he died for our sins, was buried, rose again bodily on the third day, and is the rightful King of the universe. This is the good news of the Bible, and it's the message we must believe to be saved. Paul said, "For if you confess with your mouth that Jesus is Lord and believe in your heart that God raised him from the dead, you will be saved. For it is by believing in your heart that you are made right with God, and it is by confessing with your mouth that you are saved" (Romans 10:9-10).

This then takes us back to the meaning of faith. Believing in Jesus prompts us to turn away from our old ways of life and entrust our lives to him as our Rescuer and Master. In the Bible, Jesus didn't use the word *faith* at all in his favorite invitation for people to believe in him. He simply called out, "Come, follow me." When we believe in the risen Lord, that is exactly what we do. From that moment forward, we become Christ followers. Faith isn't just an assent to facts. Nor is it a one-time decision. Real faith, biblical faith, results in a changed life as we pattern our steps after Jesus'. Habakkuk said, "The righteous will *live* [behave, make choices] by their faith" (Habakkuk 2:4, emphasis added). "Faith that doesn't show itself by good deeds," Jesus' brother said in James 2:17, "is dead."

What then does a life of faith look like? That question is the subject of the next chapter.

Faith into Life

For two thousand years believers have been asking, if all we have to do to be made right with God is believe, what are we supposed to do with all the commands in the Bible? Saying we are saved by faith and then springing a bunch of dos and don'ts on us feels like the old bait and switch. Is this Christian life about faith or works? Law or grace? The relationship between faith and action lies at the heart of practical theology.

Law and Grace, Faith and Works

Most Americans who have had little exposure to the Bible have at least heard of the Ten Commandments. Whether through Charlton Heston setting the children of Israel free every spring when Cecil B. DeMille's classic makes its annual pilgrimage to network television, or through the media coverage of controversies about courthouse displays, most people at least know the Bible contains commandments. That doesn't necessarily mean they could name more than one or two, but they know they exist. And most people assume living a life that pleases God has something to do with keeping them.

Yet the good news of Jesus tells us that a way of being made right with God now exists outside of keeping a list like the Ten Commandments. Paul insisted,

> But now God has shown us a different way of being made right in his sight—not by obeying the law but by the way promised in the Scriptures long ago. We are made right in God's sight when we trust in Jesus Christ to take away our sins. And we can all be saved in this same way, no matter who we are or *what we have done.* (Romans 3:21-22, emphasis added)

In Galatians 3:11, Paul added that no one will ever be made right by keeping the Law. Obeying the Ten Commandments won't earn anything for us in God's sight. In fact, once we come to Christ, we are dead to the Law (see Romans 7:4-6). We've been released from it.

Does this then mean we are free to break the Law if we are no longer under its power? Not at all. Being free in Christ doesn't mean a freedom to sin, but rather a freedom *from* sin. We didn't just die to the Law. We also died to sin (see Romans 6:2). We are no longer under its power. We don't have to follow those urges that well up inside us. Jesus' death and resurrection set us free to live a life that pleases God.

Some people assume our freedom in Christ means we don't have to do anything for God whatsoever. James, writing to believers who had come out of Judaism, addressed this issue. His readers knew all about the Law and felt grateful to be out from under it. Yet they jumped to the conclusion that now that Jesus had come, they didn't have to do a thing. James confronted this attitude when he wrote, "Dear brothers and sisters, what's the use of saying you have faith if you don't prove it by your actions? That kind of faith can't save anyone" (James 2:14). Faith without works, he said, is dead.

This brings us back to where we started. If faith needs works to be real, doesn't that mean we still have to keep God's rules? Paul addressed this question in both Galatians and Colossians. In Colossians 2:20-23, he wrote:

> You have died with Christ, and he has set you free from the evil powers of this world. So why do you keep on following rules of the world, such as, "Don't handle, don't eat, don't touch." Such rules are mere human

teaching about things that are gone as soon as we use them. These rules may seem wise because they require strong devotion, humility, and severe bodily discipline. But they have no effect when it comes to conquering a person's evil thoughts and desires.

Some object, saying that laying aside all rules leads to a lax life of sin. Paul's solution is simple. Rather than following rules, he told his readers to set their sights on the reality of heaven and live out the resurrection life believers have in Christ (see Colossians 3:1-2). How? By putting to death whatever remains of the sinful things lurking in us, things such as self-absorption, envy, lust, and greed. In their place, we are to put on Christ's nature so that our minds and actions are full of generosity, patience, forgiveness, and love (see Colossians 3:12-14).

Colossians isn't the only place Paul confronted rule makers. The Galatian believers started off strong in faith but were led astray by some teachers from Jerusalem. These teachers said faith in Christ was enough to get you started in the God life, but if you really meant business with God, you had to keep the Law of Moses. This line of teaching turns up today when groups lay down a set of rules that all "real" Christians keep, rules like no dancing, no television, no movies, no caffeine, and no anything else you can imagine.

To understand how serious an issue this is, you need to read Galatians in its entirety. Paul's response to legalism basically comes down to this: We are not under the law; we are under grace. The Christian life isn't about keeping rules but about following Christ by faith. Does this mean we are free to break all the rules and the Bible's commandments don't apply to us? Not necessarily. Following Christ by faith means love, not selfish sin.

A life that seeks to love God and others is the very opposite of sin. To the degree that the commandments describe a life of love, they are useful trainers.

But if we treat them as mere rules to follow through willpower, we misuse them. No amount of willpower is ever enough. Yet even then, the commandments are valuable for teaching us how far we are from God and for stripping away our delusions of self-righteousness. Paul explained:

> [The Law's] purpose was to make obvious to everyone that we are, in ourselves, out of right relationship with God, and therefore to show us the futility of devising some religious system for getting by our own efforts what we can only get by waiting in faith for God to complete his promise. For if any kind of rule-keeping had power to create life in us, we would certainly have gotten it by this time. Until the time when we were mature enough to respond freely in faith to the living God, we were carefully surrounded and protected by the Mosaic law. The law was like those Greek tutors, with which you are familiar, who escort children to school and protect them from danger or distraction, making sure the children will really get to the place they set out for. But now you have arrived at your destination: By faith in Christ you are in direct relationship with God. (Galatians 3:22-26, MSG)

Living by faith places us under obligation to a new law, the law of love. Paul went on: "For when we place our faith in Christ Jesus, it makes no difference to God whether we are circumcised or not circumcised. What is important is faith expressing itself in love" (Galatians 5:6). As we seek to follow Christ by faith and express that trust in him through love, our lives will overflow with love toward God and others.

Sin, then, can be defined as any act that does not express faith in Christ, love for God, and love for others. This sets a much higher standard than mere rule keeping. But the laws of the Bible remain useful guides for expressing love toward God and other people.

Loving God

The first and greatest commandment, the one upon which all the rest hang, is found in Deuteronomy 6:5: "You must love the LORD your God with all your heart, all your soul, and all your strength." Faith that expresses itself through love begins here, with loving God. But what else would we expect? God's love for us is what drove him to reach out to us in the first place. It started in the mercy he showed when he made provision for the first man and woman's sin, when he carried Noah's family in the ark, and when he promised to make Abraham and Sarah into a great nation. God put his love on display when he led the Israelites out of Egypt and during the centuries of their sin through the rest of the Old Testament period. Then he expressed his love in a way that people haven't been able to comprehend even two thousand years later, as he hung his Son on a cross for us.

If we believe all of this to be true, we will respond by loving God in return. How can we express love to someone we can't see, hear, or touch? The Bible gives us three ways.

1. We love God by keeping his commandments.

Jesus drew a connection between loving God and doing what he asks of us. He told his disciples, "Those who obey my commandments are the ones who love me" (John 14:21). Many years later John wrote, "Loving God means keeping his commandments, and really, that isn't difficult. For every child of God defeats this evil world by trusting Christ to give the victory" (1 John 5:3-4).

This might seem like we're right back where we started, right back to keeping rules to keep God happy. But that's not the case at all. Showing love through obedience is entirely different from trying to earn love with obedience. God is our Father, which means we need to see this concept through the lens of a family. When a little boy wakes up early on a Saturday morning and starts vacuuming the living room because he wants to surprise his mother (even though she would rather sleep in than be jolted awake by the sound of the vacuum cleaner), we smile and say how cute. The boy just wants to show his mother he loves her. However, if a little boy wakes up early and starts doing chores because he is afraid his mom or dad will kick him out of the house if he doesn't, that's a tragedy.

Too many people approach obeying God like the latter instead of the former. But if we are children who have been overwhelmed by his love, we want to find a way to show him love in return. When we hear him say in his Word, "Go feed the hungry," or "Pray for a sick friend," or "Tell a neighbor about my Son," we want to go and do it, not because we have to, but because it gives us a way to express love to God. That's what it means to show God love by keeping his commands.

When we approach obedience in this way, we make an amazing discovery. John said keeping God's commands isn't that difficult. Anyone who has tried to keep the Law would disagree. But we aren't trying to keep the Law. Instead, as we show love to God by doing whatever will put a smile on his face, we find that his Spirit inside us enables us to do what we could never do on our own. Philippians 2:13 promises, "For God is working in you, giving you the desire to obey him and the power to do what pleases him." As a result, acts of obedience become acts of faith. Rather than trying to muster up the strength to do something great for God, we trust him and rely on his strength as he works through us. Then faith truly does express itself in love, which results in obedience.

2. We love God by loving other people.

We can't see God. We can't touch him with our hands or connect with him in the physical realm. Yet the Bible tells us we can express love to him in this physical world by loving those he made in his image. John said, "Everyone who loves the Father love his children, too" (1 John 5:1). Jesus said the second greatest commandment is to love our neighbors as ourselves (see Matthew 22:39). He went so far as to say that whenever we show love to others through feeding the hungry, caring for strangers, clothing the naked, and visiting the sick and prisoners, we are in fact showing love to him. He told his disciples, "I assure you, when you did it to one of the least of these my brothers and sisters, you were doing it to me!" (Matthew 25:40).

God is love. It only stands to reason that his children will love as well. Jesus said our love for one another will prove to the world that we are his disciples (see John 13:35). In fact, it's impossible to love God and not love those he made in his image. "If someone says, 'I love God,' but hates a Christian brother or sister, that person is a liar," John explained, "for if we don't love people we can see, how can we love God, whom we have not seen?" (1 John 4:20). Loving others must be more than some warm, fuzzy feeling. Throughout the Bible the Lord tells us to stand up for those who cannot stand up for themselves, upholding justice and defending the oppressed (see James 1:27; Micah 6:8). Loving God by loving people means addressing practical needs. John said, "But if anyone has enough money to live well and sees a brother or sister in need and refuses to help—how can God's love be in that person?" (1 John 3:17). When we love others, we pray for them, share our lives with them, and carry their burdens (see Galatians 6:2).

3. We express love to God through worship.

When you love someone, you tell him or her. You can't stop yourself. The more his or her love grips your heart, the more the words just slip out. When it comes to God, these expressions of love are called worship. Worship is more than singing songs along with a bunch of other people in a church building. It's an act where God's children tell him how much he means to them. That's what's going on in heaven right now. Revelation 4–5 gives us a peek into heaven, where everyone and everything are gathered around God's throne singing love songs to him. They're telling him he is wonderful and beautiful and mighty. That's worship.

For some people, expressing love verbally doesn't come naturally. That's not a problem. The book of Psalms is filled with love songs to our Savior that we can make our own. Psalm 18 is a great example. The psalmist began, "I love you, LORD; you are my strength," and then he went on to tell God why he loved him. He told how the Lord rescued him from his enemies and came through when hope was lost. Psalm 8 was written in a quiet moment when the psalmist sat under a night sky and felt overwhelmed by the beauty surrounding him.

Love has to be expressed. God tells us he loves us whenever we take the time to listen. He constantly pours out expressions of his love on us. And when we accept his love, we will want to reciprocate. Faith expresses itself in love by bowing down and worshiping the God who loves us with a love greater than our minds can imagine.

These three principles—loving God through obedience, through loving others, and by living a life of worship—will guide us even in the gray areas of life. Whenever we are unsure what to do or whether an action is right or wrong, we need to ask what faith expressing itself in love would lead us to do. Has God given specific instructions about the course of action we are considering? Will our actions express love to other people, or will they tear other people down—or even make them stumble in their journeys with God? And finally, will the course of action we are considering bring glory to God? We don't have to try to find all the answers on our own. Colossians 3:16 says, "Let the words of Christ, in all their richness, live in your hearts and make you wise." As we let God's words fill us, and as we seek to honor God in all we do, he will direct our paths.

True Community

When God made the universe, he stepped back after each phase of creation and declared, "This is good." However, he found one thing that wasn't good even before sin entered the picture. In Genesis 2:18 he declared, "It is not good for the man to be alone." These words refer to more than the first man's need for a woman. They give us our first hint that when God designed human beings, he meant for us to be communal creatures. We are designed to connect with other people in relationships. We need to live in community with other people.

Community Lost

Living in harmony may have been easy before the Fall, but it's been anything but since. When Los Angeles erupted in violent riots on April 29, 1992, after a mostly white jury acquitted four white police officers of the videotaped beating of a black man named Rodney King, King himself stood before the city and tearfully asked, "Can't we all just get along?" Sadly, human history suggests the answer is no. Sin strikes at the heart of community, tearing it apart and separating us from one another. It's not just acts of violence that have been a part of life since one of Adam and Eve's sons killed his brother. Our sinful natures pull us into ourselves and away from others.

Sin doesn't just separate us from God; it also builds a barrier between us and those made in God's image. You can see the wall going up in Genesis 3 when God confronted the first man and woman over their sin. God asked Adam a simple question: "Have you eaten the fruit I commanded you not to eat?" (Genesis 3:11). The first words out of Adam's mouth were *yes, but . . .* as in, yes, I ate the fruit, but it wasn't my fault. He told

God, "It was the woman you gave me who brought me the fruit, and I ate it" (Genesis 3:12). The Bible doesn't record the conversation Adam and Eve had later, but it probably went something like this:

> *Eve:* Yeah, thanks for telling God this whole eating the forbidden fruit thing was *my* idea. You didn't have to eat it, you know. And why didn't you do anything about the flipping talking snake before things went too far?
>
> *Adam:* Me! Why are you blaming me?! You pulled the fruit off the tree and took a bite. I told you what God said about it, but nooooooooo, you didn't listen. You just had to taste it for yourself.
>
> *Eve:* That's just like you, throwing all the blame on me. You make me sick.
>
> *Adam:* Well, that goes double for me, forbidden fruit picker.
>
> *Eve:* Buck passer.
>
> *Adam:* Drop dead.
>
> *Eve:* You drop dead. I wish I had a mother, 'cause I'd go home to her right now.

If they didn't have this exact conversation, they probably had something close to it. That's what sin does to people. It turns us against one another. As sin progressed through history, the walls between people grew higher and higher. With time, hating certain people became part of the human psyche. Even though all of us are made in God's image, and even though every person on the planet shares common ancestors (which means we are all part of the same family), we look down on people and hate them because they were born with a different amount of dermal melanin, or because they were born in a different place than us, or because they wear clothes from Wal-Mart rather than Abercrombie & Fitch, or vice versa.

Saved into Community

When Jesus rose again, he undid the effects of the Fall, not just in the lives of individuals, but also in our relationships with others. He reconciles us not only to God, but also to one another. This isn't a peripheral part of his work on the cross. Jesus died both to save individuals from their sins and to restore them into the type of community for which God designed them. The Bible calls this community the church. In Ephesians 5:23-30, Paul explained how Jesus gave his life for this collective community, to become her Savior. He didn't just sacrifice himself to save individuals. We cannot separate the salvation we receive as individuals from the community of which this salvation makes us a part.

The community Jesus died to save encompasses all of the redeemed across time and space, as well as local groups of believers. The first is called the universal church, the second the local church. As a part of the universal church, we are part of a community that stretches back to the beginning of time, wraps around the world, and will last throughout all of eternity. We share a connection with believers who lived centuries ago, as well as with Christ followers who live on the other side of the globe today. In Christ, God has interconnected our lives with theirs. Local gatherings of this community make this connection more than an esoteric truth. As we experience community within the local church, our lives truly become intertwined with others who've entered this new birth.

The New Testament uses several word pictures for this community. One of the most curious shows how inseparable from this community our lives become after we're saved. Paul wrote, "We have all been baptized into Christ's body by one Spirit, and we have all received the same Spirit" (1 Corinthians 12:13). The word *body* doesn't just mean a collected group of people like the student body of a school. In this passage, body means body as in a human body. Paul described how together we are Christ's body, and all of us are different parts. Some of us are feet; some are hands. Others are eyes or ears. Just as our human bodies work best when every member is present and working the way God designed it, so too Christ's body needs all of us to be connected and doing what God designed us to do.

This connection is more than one of function. We grow spiritually through our connection to the rest of the body. Paul told the Colossians, "For we are joined together in his body by his strong sinews, and we grow only as we get our nourishment and strength from God" (Colossians 2:19). Our spiritual lives depend on our connection to his body just as the parts of our physical bodies need to stay connected to us to survive. An eyeball wouldn't last long if it decided it was sick of being stuck in someone's head and wanted to live on its own. That's why horror movies are the only place you see hands crawling around on their own without being connected to an arm. Hands and eyes need to stay put if they are to remain healthy and strong, just as believers must stay connected to the local expressions of the community of faith called the church for their spiritual health.

Family Ties

The interrelationships within the church go beyond the interaction of hands and feet and eyes and ears. In addition to the picture of the church as Christ's body, the Bible also calls this community the family of God. Paul wrote, "Long ago, even before he made the world, God loved us and chose us in Christ to be holy and without fault in his eyes. His unchanging plan has always been to adopt us into his own family by bringing us to himself through Jesus Christ. And this gave him great pleasure" (Ephesians 1:4-5). As God's children, we have the pleasure of calling God our Father and drawing near to him anytime we like. But that's not the only reason God brings us into his family. He adopts us as sons and daughters, and in the process, he gives us a bunch of brothers and sisters to love.

This family is now the place where we are to fulfill the "one another" verses in the Bible, such as love one another (see John 13:34), pray for one another (see James 5:16), share one another's troubles (see Galatians 6:1-2), honor one another (see Romans 12:10), get along with one another (see Romans 12:16), forgive one another (see Ephesians 4:32), consider one another to be more important than ourselves (see Philippians 2:3), and encourage one another (see 1 Thessalonians 5:11). Doing all of the above isn't a burden. Instead, these acts should flow out of the love we have for one another, love that flows through us from our Father. The "one anothers" are, according to Jesus, both the test and the evidence of our relationship with him (see John 13:35).

Why is all of this necessary? Why does God make such a big deal about our relationships in his family? Stanley Grenz and John Franke explained it this way:

> [At] the heart of our understanding of the church is the realization that our human calling is to reflect the character of God. Of course, there may well be a personal aspect to this human destiny. Nevertheless, because God is ultimately none other than the divine Trinitarian persons-in-relationship, a relationship characterized by a mutuality that can only be described as love, the *imago dei* [image of God] is ultimately human persons-in-loving-relationships as well. Only in relationship — as persons-in-community — are we able to reflect the fullness of divine character. And because the company of Jesus' disciples is called to be the divine image, the church is essentially a community characterized by love, a people who reflect in relation to one another and to all creation the character of the Creator.[2]

When we live out the "one anothers" through loving relationships within God's family, we put God's character on display for the world to see. The goal isn't just to be noticed. Rather, the sight of true community stirs the image of God within those who don't yet know Christ. They find themselves drawn toward that which they were made to experience. As they draw closer, they hear the good news of Jesus and see it lived out in his family.

The Beautiful Bride

The Bible also portrays the church's relationship to Christ as a bride and bridegroom. The Old Testament prophets first used this analogy to describe the Lord's relationship with Israel and Judah. However, in the Prophets, this relationship had gone awry. The Lord's beautiful bride had run off in search of other lovers and turned herself into a prostitute. Yet, in spite of her unfaithfulness, the Lord told her he would take her back.[3]

You need to keep this Old Testament imagery in mind to fully appreciate the way the New Testament now describes the church as the bride of Christ. Paul wrote, "[Christ] gave up his life for her to make her holy and clean, washed by baptism and God's word. He did this to present her to himself as a glorious church without spot or wrinkle or any other blemish. Instead, she will be holy and without fault" (Ephesians 5:25-27). This is who we are in this community called the church. We are the holy bride Jesus passionately loves. The Bible promises that one day soon the Bridegroom will return for us. Then we will spend all of eternity in his presence, loving him and being loved in return.

The last picture we have of this bride in the Bible comes on the very last page. Revelation 22:17 says, "The Spirit and the bride say, 'Come.' Let each one who hears them say, 'Come.' Let the thirsty ones come—anyone who wants to. Let them come and drink the water of life without charge." As the bride of Christ, part of our job is to constantly invite people to come and experience what we've found in Christ. This fellowship we enjoy with one another and with Jesus is open to anyone. This should be the one place where every wall sin builds between people is broken down. Race, gender, national origin, economic class, and anything else you can imagine — none of it matters. All that matters is a thirst for God. The bride now invites all who feel this longing, all who hear the Spirit calling them to Christ, to come join the family and experience God's grace for themselves.

QUESTIONS

Can salvation be lost?

The argument usually goes something like this. Someone fires away a statement like, "You people who believe in 'once saved always saved,' you think all someone has to do is walk down an aisle and give his life to Jesus, and then he can go out and sin all he wants. It doesn't matter what he does after that. He can drink and cuss—heck, he could even go out and kill someone—and according to your theology, he would still go to heaven when he dies! I don't see that in the Bible."

The usual response is something along the lines of, "You people who think you can lose your salvation say all you have to do to be saved is believe, but then you tell people they better work hard or God's going to kick them out of his family. Yeah, it's saved by faith and kept by works. And for that matter, how much sin does it take to lose your salvation? Does anyone really know? Of course not. You never know if you are saved or lost, and you end up having to get resaved every other week. I don't see that in the Bible."

So who is right? Can a person lose his salvation? Is it possible to be part of God's family with a guaranteed spot in heaven today, only to lose it tomorrow? The answers to these questions fall into two primary positions, Calvinist and Arminian. The former believes the gift of salvation can never be lost, while the latter believes it can.

Before we dive into the debate, we need to remember one important truth. Walking with Christ isn't like a world history class. Our goal should be to please God in *everything* we do, not to figure out the bare minimum we need to do to get a passing grade. Often that is the real motivation for people who ask whether or not we are secure in Christ. For them, the question should read, "How little can I do for God before he kicks me out of his family?" That attitude not only misses the point of the debate, but it also fails to grasp what it means to follow Christ by faith.

The Calvinist Position

The Westminster Confession of Faith, an English Calvinist doctrinal statement written in 1647, declares, "They, whom God has accepted in His Beloved, effectually called, and sanctified by His Spirit, can neither totally nor finally fall away from the state of grace, but shall certainly persevere therein to the end, and be eternally saved." Other groups use different language, but this remains the Calvinist answer to the question. The Confession goes on to explain that the perseverance of the saints doesn't depend on our ability or willpower, but on God. According to this view, our salvation began when God chose us unconditionally before the foundation of the world (see Ephesians 1:4-8). Jesus died specifically for those God chose (see Matthew 26:28), and his Spirit drew them with a grace that no one can resist (see John 6:44). We didn't add anything to this before we were saved, because we were completely dead in our sin (see Romans 5:12), and we can't take anything from it after we are saved, because it is all God's work. Given all that God has done to save us, he will not now let us go.

This position points to many promises in the Bible that seem to guarantee our salvation. Paul said,

> And I am convinced that nothing can ever separate us from his love. Death can't, and life can't. The angels can't, and the demons can't. Our fears for today, our worries about tomorrow, and even the powers of hell can't keep

God's love away. Whether we are high above the sky or in the deepest ocean, nothing in all creation will ever be able to separate us from the love of God that is revealed in Christ Jesus our Lord. (Romans 8:38-39)

For Calvinists, if nothing can separate us from God's love, then nothing can separate us from him. Jesus promised, "My sheep recognize my voice; I know them, and they follow me. I give them eternal life, and they will never perish. No one will snatch them away from me, for my Father has given them to me, and he is more powerful than anyone else. So no one can take them from me" (John 10:27-29).

Our security in Christ doesn't mean we somehow become impervious to sin. We still face temptation, yet God gives us the power to overcome it. Paul said,

But remember that the temptations that come into your life are no different from what others experience. And God is faithful. He will keep the temptation from becoming so strong that you can't stand up against it. When you are tempted, he will show you a way out so that you will not give in to it. (1 Corinthians 10:13)

If we do fall to temptation, that doesn't mean God will disown us. First John 1:8-9 promises, "If we say we have no sin, we are only fooling ourselves and refusing to accept the truth. But if we confess our sins to him, he is faithful and just to forgive us and to cleanse us from every wrong."

King David is the classic example of a godly man who not only fell into sin, but also committed acts unthinkable for one who claimed to know God, including adultery and murder.

Yet when he confessed his sin, God forgave him. God didn't disown him. He refused to leave David in his sinful condition and sent the prophet Nathan to confront him.

God's willingness to forgive shouldn't be mistaken for a license to sin. Some people believe the permanently saved position teaches that once you have your ticket to heaven punched, you can live like the Devil without consequence. That's not the case. When a person has been born again, his life will change. Paul said we become new creatures in Christ (see 2 Corinthians 5:17). Calvinists acknowledge that not everyone who makes a profession of faith at some point in his life has truly been born again. Jesus' story of the farmer planting his seed indicates this (see Luke 8:4-15). When those who have been born again drift away from God, the Spirit inside them convicts them as God pulls them back to himself.

Calvinists admit there are passages in the Bible that appear to teach that believers can lose their salvation. At the top of the list is Hebrews 6:4-6, which says,

> For it is impossible to restore to repentance those who were once enlightened — those who have experienced the good things of heaven and shared in the Holy Spirit, who have tasted the goodness of the word of God and the power of the age to come — and who then turn away from God. It is impossible to bring such people to repentance again because they are nailing the Son of God to the cross again by rejecting him, holding him up to public shame.

As we will see in a moment, Arminians point to this verse as proof that salvation can be lost. However, Calvinists reply that this only appears to be the case. Millard Erickson emphasized Hebrews 6:9, which says, "Dear friends, even though we are talking like this, we really don't believe that it applies to you. We are confident that you are meant for better things, things that come with salvation." Erickson explained, "There is a logical possibility of apostasy, but it will not come to pass in the case of believers. Although they could abandon their faith and consequently come to the fate described in Hebrews 6, the grace of God prevents them from apostasizing. God does this, not by making it impossible for believers to fall away, but by making it certain they will not."[4]

The Arminian Position

The Arminian position is best summarized by the Free Methodist Church's "Articles of Religion":

> Christians can sin willfully and sever their relationship with Christ. Even so by repentance before God, forgiveness is granted and the relationship with Christ restored, for not every sin is the sin against the Holy Spirit and unpardonable. God's grace is sufficient for those who truly repent and, by His enabling, amend their lives. However, forgiveness does not give believers liberty to sin and escape the consequences of sinning. God has given responsibility and power to the church to restore penitent believers through loving reproof, counsel, and acceptance.[5]

This belief that someone can forfeit her salvation grows out of the overall Arminian understanding of the salvation process and our role in it. Like Calvinists, Arminians believe people are dead in their sins outside Christ. However, they believe God gives what John Wesley called prevenient grace, which is "the grace that begins to enable one to choose further to cooperate with saving grace. By offering the will the restored capacity to respond to grace, the person then may freely and increasingly become an active, willing participant in receiving the conditions for justification."[6] This grace is available to all.

Arminians also believe God's choice of those who will be saved is conditional. God chooses those whom he foresees will in fact choose Jesus Christ of their own free will. Unlike Calvinists, they do not believe Jesus' atonement is limited in any way. God so loved the world that he gave his only Son to die for everyone (see John 3:16). While Arminians believe the Holy Spirit draws people to God, they believe people can, in fact, resist his advances. Peter said God wants everyone to be saved (see 2 Peter 3:9), yet we know not everyone says yes to Christ. Therefore God's grace can be refused.

All of this then leads to the Arminian position on the permanence of salvation. If a person can't be saved by God unless that person chooses by his own will to be saved, then the same person can't continue in salvation unless he chooses to. In other words, you can choose to walk away from God, and he will let you go.

Like Calvinists, Arminians find ample support for their position in the Bible. Hebrews 2:1-3 warns,

> So we must listen very carefully to the truth we have heard, or we may drift away from it. The message God delivered through angels has always proved true, and the people were punished for every violation of the law and every act of disobedience. What makes us think that we

can escape if we are indifferent to this great salvation
that was announced by the Lord Jesus himself?

They also point to Hebrews 6:4-6 (cited earlier) as proof that
people can fall away. In the Arminian system, this passage
doesn't describe a theoretical falling away, but a fact that indeed
happens. Examples, they say, abound in the Bible, including
King Saul and Judas.

Although this position is named after James Arminius, his
own writings indicate he may not have been a full-fledged
Arminian. On the subject of perseverance he wrote:

> Though I here openly and ingenuously affirm, I never
> taught that a true believer can, either totally or finally fall
> away from the faith, and perish; yet I will not conceal,
> that there are passages of scripture which seem to me
> to wear this aspect; and those answers to them which I
> have been permitted to see, are not of such a kind as to
> approve themselves on all points to my understanding.
> On the other hand, certain passages are produced for the
> contrary doctrine [of unconditional perseverance] which
> are worthy of much consideration.[7]

The most influential Arminian, the man who propelled
this doctrine to the status it enjoys today, was John Wesley.
Wesley didn't couch the arguments in theological talk. Instead,
he brought the doctrine down to a practical level with stories
such as this:

> Satan summoned his powers, and examined what mischief
> each of them had done. One said, "I have set a house on

fire, and destroyed all its inhabitants." Another said, "I have raised a storm at sea, and sunk a ship; and all on board perished in the waters." Satan answered, "Perhaps those that were burnt or drowned were saved." A third said, "I have been forty years tempting a holy man to commit adultery; and I have left him asleep in his sin." Hearing this, Satan rose to do him honour; and all hell resounded with his praise. Hear this, all ye that imagine you cannot fall from grace![8]

Wesley also answered the question of whether or not those who fall from grace can, in fact, be saved again if they repent. He wrote:

If it be asked, "Do any real apostates find mercy from God? Do any that have 'made shipwreck of faith and a good conscience,' recover what they have lost? Do you know, have you seen, any instance of persons who found redemption in the blood of Jesus, and afterwards fell away, and yet were restored,—'renewed again to repentance'?" Yea, verily; and not one, or an hundred only, but, I am persuaded, several thousands. . . . Innumerable are the instances of this kind, of those who had fallen, but now stand upright. Indeed, it is so far from being an uncommon thing for a believer to fall and be restored, that it is rather uncommon to find any believers who are not conscious of having been backsliders from God, in a higher or lower degree, and perhaps more than once, before they were established in faith.[9]

Somewhere In Between

This issue doesn't leave room for a sort-of-one or sort-of-the-other answer. Either you believe a person can lose his or her salvation, or you believe God keeps us safe forever. However, there are those who believe salvation cannot be lost but who do not want to identify themselves as Calvinist. Many Baptists believe in what they call "the security of the believer," while rejecting the rest of the Calvinist teachings on salvation, such as unconditional election, limited atonement, and irresistible grace. On these questions, their views would come closer to Arminians.

What's the deal with baptism?

Jesus' final words to his disciples were, "Go and make disciples of all the nations, baptizing them in the name of the Father and the Son and the Holy Spirit. Teach these new disciples to obey all the commands I have given you. And be sure of this: I am with you always, even to the end of the age" (Matthew 28:19-20). These instructions, commonly called the Great Commission, link the spread of the good news with the rite of baptism. According to Jesus, the two go hand in hand. As a result, virtually all Christian groups practice some form of baptism.

Although most churches baptize, they do it in very different ways and for very different reasons. Most use water, but some sprinkle, others pour, and still others dunk people completely under. Some churches baptize infants, while others baptize only those old enough to make a personal decision to follow Jesus. Quakers don't baptize with water at all. Catholics and Lutherans call baptism a sacrament — that is, a means of conveying grace. Reformed churches and Presbyterians call it a sign and seal of the covenant God makes with us, comparable to the Old Testament practice of circumcision. Baptists, and other groups that practice believer's baptism, see it as a sign or an outward witness of one's decision to turn to Jesus.

How can these groups do so many different things all under the banner of baptism? While we will deal with the who, why, and how of baptism as three separate questions, all three are intertwined within each church's understanding of this rite. Why dunkers dunk and who they dunk are tied together. The same goes for churches that sprinkle infants.

What Does Baptism Mean?

Catholics call baptism the "door to the church" or "the door to the sacraments" for "by it we are made members of Christ and incorporated with the Church."[10] Both new converts and children are to receive this sacrament. Yet the act of baptism doesn't just unite a person with the church; it is a means by which God's grace is conferred and removes the stain of original sin. The roots of this belief go back to Augustine, who wrote in the fifth century:

> Inasmuch as the generation of sinful flesh through the one man, Adam, draws into condemnation all who are born of such generation, so the generation of the Spirit of grace through the one man Jesus Christ, draws to the justification of eternal life all who, because predestinated, partake of this regeneration. But the sacrament of baptism is undoubtedly the sacrament of regeneration. . . . Even an infant, therefore, must be imbued with the sacrament of regeneration, lest without it his would be an unhappy exit out of this life; and this baptism is not administered except for the remission of sins.[11]

However, this baptism does not remove sins committed after it is conferred. Those who are baptized as babies must also then continue on in the faith.

Protestants who view baptism as a sacrament differ from Catholics on their understanding of who receives grace from it. Rather than seeing baptism as a means by which God's grace is given absolutely, Protestants emphasize faith as a prerequisite. Only then will the waters of baptism have any effect. Martin Luther put it this way:

Water doesn't make these things happen, of course. It is God's Word, which is with and in the water. Because, without God's Word, the water is plain water and not baptism. But with God's Word it is a Baptism, a grace-filled water of life, a bath of new birth in the Holy Spirit, as St. Paul said to Titus in the third chapter: "Through this bath of rebirth and renewal of the Holy Spirit, which He poured out on us abundantly through Jesus Christ, our Savior, that we, justified by the same grace are made heirs according to the hope of eternal life. This is a faithful saying."[12]

Luther taught that not only do new believers need to be baptized, but also infants. How can a baby show the faith required for baptism? Those holding this view offer two possible solutions. First, the infant may possess an unconscious faith. For evidence they point to John the Baptist, who was filled with the Holy Spirit even in his mother's womb (see Luke 1:15). The second solution simply says that the faith of the parents is enough. The child then believes vicariously through his parents, but will need to make a decision on his own when he reaches a sufficient age.[13]

Presbyterian and Reformed churches also emphasize faith, yet they see baptism as the New Testament equivalent of circumcision. Rather than removing original sin or bestowing faith vicariously, baptism is a sign of the new covenant God makes with his children through Christ. Baptism signifies entering into this covenant and receiving God's gift of salvation. Just as circumcision symbolized the cutting away of sin and a change of heart, baptism pictures the washing away of sin in this new relationship with God. Because God's old covenant extended to the children of believers, infants and children should also be baptized. However, faith is still required of a child once he is old enough to understand the gospel. The act of baptism alone does not secure salvation.

Finally, other churches practice believer's baptism—that is, they only baptize those who have personally made a decision to follow Christ. Most of these churches also practice immersion, although some pour water over the candidate's head. This view's understanding of baptism is taken from Romans 6:4, which uses baptism as a picture of the transformation that takes place when a person receives Christ as Savior. It says, "For we died and were buried with Christ by baptism. And just as Christ was raised from the dead by the glorious power of the Father, now we also may live new lives." Believer's baptism, especially by immersion, reenacts this verse. As the candidate is lowered into the water, we see her death and burial with Christ. Then, as she is raised out of the water, we see her spiritual resurrection with Christ to a new life. In this view, baptism is a public way of confessing one's faith in Christ and the decision to follow him. While most say that baptism isn't required to be saved, they do maintain that it's the first step of the new walk as a disciple of Jesus, following him in a first act of obedience.

Who Should Be Baptized?

The question of who should be baptized comes down to a more basic question: Should infants be baptized? A majority of churches in the world and in history answer with an emphatic yes. They base this answer not just on centuries of practice, but also on several key passages in the Bible. In the New Testament, entire households were baptized together (see Acts 16:33; 18:8; 1 Corinthians 1:16; 7:14). Although the Bible doesn't specifically say young children and infants were included, it doesn't exclude them. Jesus himself rebuked his disciples when they tried to keep little children from bothering him. He said, "Let the children come to me. Don't stop them! For the Kingdom of Heaven belongs to such as these" (Matthew 19:14).

Those who reject infant baptism base their arguments on the New Testament passages that show baptism to be an outward expression of one's own faith. Peter said, "Baptism is not a removal of dirt from your body; it is an appeal to God from a clean conscience" (1 Peter 3:21). This view asks, how can a baby make an appeal to God from a clean conscience? The pattern in the book of Acts also shows that baptism follows the act of personally believing in Jesus. Acts 2:41 says those who believed were baptized. Nowhere does the Bible command the baptism of babies or the very young. This view also rejects the idea that the baptized households had to include some young children, as the text doesn't say so.

Should We Dunk, Sprinkle, or Pour?

As we learned in the chapter on the baptism of the Holy Spirit, the Greek word transliterated baptize, βαπτιζω, literally means to dip, immerse, or submerge. In secular Greek the word also meant to cause to perish either by drowning or by sinking a ship.[14] Baptists and others who immerse baptismal candidates do so based on a literal understanding of the word. They also cite examples in the Bible where immersion is implied, specifically Jesus' baptism by John the Baptist. John baptized people in the Jordan River near Salim because "there was plenty of water there" (John 3:23). Matthew said that after John baptized Jesus, Jesus came up out of the water (see Matthew 3:16). It makes little sense for John to baptize in a river and for Jesus to go all the way into the water if John did little more than sprinkle or pour some water on Jesus' head. Those who immerse also point to the meaning of baptism as pictured in Romans 6:4 as an argument for immersion.

Those who sprinkle and pour say that the primary meaning of baptism is not death and resurrection but the purification from sin. This symbolism, they maintain, can be shown through any method of baptism. In fact, sprinkling may be the best way of showing this, for Ezekiel said of the new birth, "Then I will sprinkle clean water on you, and you will be clean. Your filth will be washed away, and you will no longer worship idols. I will give you a new heart with new and right desires, and I will put a new spirit in you. I will take out your stony heart of sin and give you a new, obedient heart" (Ezekiel 36:25-26). They also point out that immersion is doubtful in many of the instances where people were baptized in the Bible. For example, did the Philippian jailor leave his post to go down to the local river to be immersed? This seems unlikely.

Those who sprinkle generally agree that other modes of baptism are also valid, while those who immerse generally do not. Mennonites practice believer's baptism, but they usually pour water over the candidate's head rather than immerse.

Baptism as a Spiritual Experience

The Society of Friends, or Quakers, does not practice any sort of literal baptism with water. Quakers consider the sacrament of baptism, along with the Lord's Supper, or Communion, to be purely spiritual experiences believers enter into with Christ through worship. The real baptism is the communication of the

Holy Spirit that believers experience as they enter into God's presence. When they experience this, no other sort of baptism is needed. Quakers don't consider the observance of baptism to be wrong, but rather as simply unnecessary.

How involved should believers be in the political process?

Less than one week before the 2004 presidential election, pastor and best-selling author Rick Warren wrote an article entitled "Why every U.S. Christian must vote in this election." The article, which went out to more than 100,000 pastors and ministers via the October 27 issue of his e-newsletter, *Rick Warren's Ministry Toolbox*, opened with the line, "Tuesday, Nov. 2, will be the most important election day U.S. citizens have faced in 50 years." What made this particular election so important? Warren rightly foresaw that over the course of the next four years, more than one vacancy would open on the U.S. Supreme Court. Because justices serve lifetime terms, whoever won the election would potentially influence the direction of the United States for decades. Telling the 4 million Christians who didn't vote in the previous election that their inaction was "inexcusable," Warren told pastors, "If the members of our congregations fail to vote on Tuesday, we are actually surrendering our responsibility to choose the direction of our country for the next 40 years."

Warren was far from alone in urging Christians to vote. His church, Saddleback Church in Lake Forest, California, along with hundreds of other churches across the country, set up booths where people could register to vote. Other churches passed out voter guides that, although they didn't endorse certain candidates, listed how those running for office stood on key issues. Some voters were most concerned about the issues of abortion and homosexual marriage; for others, the war in Iraq and the plight of the poor were most important. The candidates took notice. They talked openly of religious faith and family values and spoke at churches and religious gatherings. Yet beyond the candidates, the real message that rang out from churches was that Christians have a divine duty to become involved in the political process.

A View Through Time

The question of the role of Christians in the political arena has run throughout the church's two-thousand-year history. During the first three centuries after Christ, most believers stood on the outside looking in, as a religious minority that the Roman Empire alternately persecuted and tolerated. Everything changed with the conversion of Emperor Constantine in AD 313. Christianity was not only legalized, but it also became the official state religion of Rome in 381. Religious authority and secular power became intertwined. Doctrinal questions became state issues, with the state using its power to suppress heresy and dissent. What was once a persecuted minority became a powerful majority as the West was Christianized, although the definition of what it meant to be a Christian didn't always line up with the biblical requirements of the new birth.

During the Reformation, the question of whether a Christian could serve as the magistrate—that is, should believers seek political power?—once again came to the forefront. John Calvin, perhaps the most influential of the Reformers, thought believers had a divine duty to bring their faith into the political arena. In his mind, social organizations had to reflect biblical principles. He reorganized the city government of Geneva and involved the clergy in municipal decisions. Calvin's ideas spread. Perhaps the most radical application of them came during the English Civil War when Oliver Cromwell executed the king and set out to establish God's kingdom on earth. When his Calvinist Puritans took over, he dismissed Parliament and disestablished the Church of England. The experiment didn't last. Shortly after Cromwell's death, the Puritans were ousted from power and the monarchy was reestablished.

All of this is particularly important for understanding the question of Christians and politics in the United States. Many of the settlers who came to North America from England and other parts of Europe in the seventeenth century were Puritans. Some were Separatists who wanted to escape what they considered to be a corrupt church in England. But others believed God had given them a divine mandate. In 1630, John Winthrop led a group of more than one thousand Puritan colonists to Massachusetts with the mission of creating a "City on a Hill" that would be a light to the world. He foresaw his new colony as a pilot church and state, which would create an ideal spiritual and secular community. This new community would then be a light that would save the Old World as well.[15] Winthrop compared his colonists' journey to America with the Israelites' deliverance from Egypt. In many ways, he believed the New England colonies were the New World equivalent of God's chosen people.

Winthrop's influence is still felt today. In many ways, his vision of America is the lens through which many believers understand both the role of the United States in the world and their role in our nation. Ronald Reagan spoke of Winthrop and his City on a Hill in his farewell address:

> The past few days when I've been at that window upstairs, I've thought a bit of the "shining city upon a hill." The phrase comes from John Winthrop, who wrote it to describe the America he imagined. What he imagined

was important because he was an early Pilgrim, an early freedom man. He journeyed here on what today we'd call a little wooden boat; and like the other Pilgrims, he was looking for a home that would be free. I've spoken of the shining city all my political life, but I don't know if I ever quite communicated what I saw when I said it. But in my mind it was a tall, proud city built on rocks stronger than oceans, windswept, God-blessed, and teeming with people of all kinds living in harmony and peace; a city with free ports that hummed with commerce and creativity. And if there had to be city walls, the walls had doors and the doors were open to anyone with the will and the heart to get here. That's how I saw it, and see it still.[16]

This idea that God has a divine plan for the United States that believers need to help fulfill has deep roots. You hear it every time someone speaks of America as a Christian nation whose founding fathers were all believers. By inference, those who share Winthrop's vision believe each of us must then continue this heritage and bring our faith to bear on the way our nation operates.

All of this means that the question of how involved a believer should be in shaping the policies and direction of the nation on both a national and local level is more than a biblical question. Yes, the Bible is the only authoritative voice on this and every question. However, the way we interpret the Bible in this matter is influenced by the way we see the role of Christians in American history and the lasting legacy they left for us. Those who embrace Winthrop's belief that America has been chosen by God to fulfill his unique purposes will approach faith and politics in a completely different way than those who don't. Americans aren't the first or only nation who believed God's providence had placed them at a unique place in history. However, for believers in the United States, this question is personal. This has especially proved true with the rise of what is referred to as the religious right over the past thirty-plus years.

A New Day

Christians have been speaking out on social issues and helping to set the nation's course since the founding of the United States. How Christian the founding fathers actually were is a subject for another place, but certainly believers have exercised considerable influence even without holding important public offices. Many believers, such as Charles Finney, spoke out against slavery and were leading abolitionists. Many of the leaders of the civil rights movement were not only believers, but also clergymen, including Martin Luther King Jr. Christians continue to make a difference through what Charles Colson calls "little platoons,"[17] affecting everything from the treatment of prisoners to care for the homeless to racial reconciliation.

However, most churches, especially those that identified themselves as theologically conservative, did not take an activist role in politics through most of the twentieth century. Most said their role was to preach the gospel and let the Holy Spirit change the world one person at a time. That attitude changed in the wake of the rapid change our culture experienced after World War II, culminating in the radical social upheaval of the sixties. The final blow came in the 1973 Supreme Court decision legalizing abortion. Led by men such as Jerry Falwell, Christian conservatives began to take a more active role, speaking out on issues such as abortion and the moral decline of

America. George Gallup even declared 1976 to be "the year of the evangelical" after Jimmy Carter, a professing born-again Christian, was elected to the White House.

Right, Left, Middle, or Above?

Since the early 1970s the power and influence of religious conservatives has grown. More to the point, the idea that all believers should be actively involved in making their moral voices heard has taken hold in conservative Christian circles. In most cases during this rise in power, the party with which most conservative Christians have identified is the Republican Party. Why? For many Christians, the single most important issue is eliminating abortion on demand.

Republicans have taken notice. In the summer of 2004, the Republican presidential campaign actively targeted churches and sought to organize evangelicals to get out the vote for their candidates. Democrats did much the same thing, targeting ethnic churches of groups that have historically voted Democratic, as well as churches that tended to be more liberal theologically.

Is this turn of events a good thing? Should Christians be another interest group to which politicians cater? Is this what it means for a believer to be involved in politics? Perhaps, but the approach comes with risks. John Whitehead, the founder and president of the conservative Rutherford Institute, sounded this warning to Christians in the summer of 2004:

> Unfortunately, all too often Christians wrap their religion in the flag, so to speak. For the Christian, country and faith are never synonymous, and they are not two equal loyalties. As Francis Schaeffer noted, "It must be

taught that patriotic loyalty must not be identified with Christianity." As Christians in past regimes have found, identifying with the establishment, as much of modern evangelicalism is doing, can present a grave danger — the establishment may easily become the church's enemy.

Not only is it perilous to identify with the established powers; it also negates the true mission of the church. The church is not to identify with power but to speak truth to power — even at great costs. Martyrs, past and present, testify to this.[18]

For the past two thousand years believers have spoken truth to power even when no one else would. Dietrich Bonhoeffer was among the first to speak out against Adolf Hitler and the "Führerprinzip," or leadership principle that sought a return of discipline and dignity for Germany through investing all power in a single leader, and he did so two days after Hitler came to power. Bonhoeffer and other Christian leaders continued to speak out against the Nazi Party, even at the cost of their own lives. Yet, in the end, what other choice did they have?

As followers of Christ, we find ourselves in a peculiar place in this world. The Bible tells us that we are strangers here on earth (see 1 Peter 1:1,17) and that our true citizenship lies in heaven (see Philippians 3:20). We may live in a democracy, but we serve a King whose kingdom stretches beyond all physical boundaries. Moreover, as citizens of the heavenly kingdom, we are told to stand out on this earth as salt and light (see Matthew 5:13-16). Jesus compared his followers to a city on a hill, "glowing in the night for all to see." Winthrop and Reagan borrowed this phrase from Jesus, but their meaning didn't exactly match his. The context of the passage shows that we become this city as we do good works for God's kingdom and as we stand up for those things that mean most to our Lord—issues such as life and justice and caring for the poor and oppressed (see Amos 2:6-8). The question believers then face regarding politics is not which party to join or which candidate to vote for, but how to bring God's priorities to bear on day-to-day life.

Does my gender limit what I can do for God?

Historically, men have dominated church leadership. For most of the first nineteen hundred years of church history, males occupied every position of authority from the pope in Rome down to the pastors of small Baptist churches in rural corners of Iowa. This held true for churches across the theological spectrum. However, in the twentieth century, more and more churches openly welcomed women into leadership positions. This is not to say women weren't important in church life before they could become pastors. The first witnesses of Jesus' resurrection were women, and they have played a key role in church life ever since. Yet some churches still limit the offices of pastor, elder, and even deacon to men. Why?

This question doesn't just break down between biblical liberals and conservatives, although churches that take a more lax view toward the Bible are more likely to allow women to serve as pastors. Some people who hold to the full inerrancy and infallibility of Scripture conclude that the Bible allows women pastors, while others who have the exact same view of the Bible reach a different conclusion entirely. Who is right?

Men Only

Churches and denominations that limit the offices of pastor and elder, and occasionally deacon, to men do so based on their understanding of both the scriptural qualifications for pastors, as well as God's design for the home. According to this view, the way God structured individual families is to be reflected in his larger family, the church. In individual families, God expects the husband and father to be the spiritual head of the home. Paul wrote, "You wives will submit to your husbands as you do to the Lord. For a husband is the head of his wife as Christ is the head of his body, the church; he gave his life to be her Savior. As the church submits to Christ, so you wives must submit to your husbands in everything" (Ephesians 5:22-24).

According to this view, the Bible's qualifications for pastors are to be understood in light of this pattern for the home. Paul told Timothy that an elder (the terms *pastor* and *elder* are used interchangeably in the New Testament) "must manage his own family well, with children who respect and obey him. For if a man cannot manage his own household, how can he take care of God's church?" (1 Timothy 3:4-5). Managing his family well implies that those who lead the church must also lead their homes, which is, according to the passage from Ephesians cited above, a responsibility God lays on men.

While some would say that 1 Timothy 3 doesn't specifically exclude women from leadership positions, the same cannot be said of 1 Timothy 2:11-15. There Paul wrote:

> Women should listen and learn quietly and submissively. I do not let women teach men or have authority over them. Let them listen quietly. For God made Adam first, and afterward he made Eve. And it was the woman, not Adam, who was deceived by Satan, and sin was the result. But women will be saved through childbearing and by continuing to live in faith, love, holiness, and modesty.

Teaching men as well as women and exercising authority over both sexes are key responsibilities of pastors. If women can't do these things, how then can they hold this office? Paul expressed virtually the same thing in 1 Corinthians 14:34-35. Those holding this view believe these passages close the book on the question.

One of the chief objections against this position is that it neglects the abilities God gives people of both sexes. If God gives these gifts, he obviously wants to see them used. However, giftedness doesn't override the Bible's clear teaching. Dorothy Patterson, a seminary professor, writes:

> I have three graduate degrees in theology—considerably more theological education than most pastors. I have experience on the public platform, and some even suggest that I have gifts for biblical exposition and teaching. Others have testified that I have met their needs through my messages. Some men have expressed appreciation for my ministry. However, ministry success, public affirmation, spousal permission, pastoral blessing, widespread opportunity—none is the biblical criterion for what I should or should not do in the kingdom of Christ. . . . Any calling I believe to be from God is filtered through my human frailties. What I *feel* may not be what God *wills*. That is why Scripture is ever the monitor and governor of all I desire to do for God.[19]

Critics also charge that this view reduces women to second-class citizens within the church. If they can't serve in every capacity, they will remain forever victims of a stained-glass ceiling. Yet proponents of this view argue that this is not the case at all. "The question at hand is not whether women are of equal value to men," says the Executive Committee of the Southern Baptist Convention, "nor is it whether they can minister effectively. They are, and they do! Nor is it an issue of the autonomy of the local church. It is, rather, that the Scripture assigns the role of pastor to males."[20] Women serve in a wide variety of roles within churches that reserve the senior pastorate to males, including paid staff positions. At the end of the day, for those holding this view, the question comes back to the Bible, and there they find a definitive answer that they believe does not change with the times.

Open to All

Those who believe the Bible allows both men and women to serve as deacons, elders, and pastors find support for their position throughout Scripture. The Old Testament includes accounts of strong women who led Israel at crucial times. Moses, the great prophet and lawgiver, was assisted by his sister, Miriam. Exodus 15:20 calls her a prophet. Deborah was both a prophet and a judge who led all of Israel (see Judges 4–5). She held court in the hill country of Ephraim and settled disputes for the Israelites. When the Canaanites attacked, she ordered Barak to lead an army of ten thousand warriors against them. He said he would do so only if she rode along with him at the head of the army.

Women also played a prominent ministry role in the New Testament. Philip had four virgin daughters who were all prophets (see Acts 21:9). Euodia and Syntyche were coworkers with Paul in spreading the gospel (see Philippians 4:2-3). Priscilla worked alongside her husband Aquila in spreading the gospel in Corinth and Ephesus. Paul called them his coworkers and usually named Priscilla first (see Romans 16:3). This may mean that she was the leader of the two, because Paul's name was always listed first when it was put in conjunction with his coworkers. Paul was the unquestioned leader of his team, and this may have been the case with Priscilla. A church met in Priscilla and Aquila's home; they may or may not have been coleaders of the group.

Those who believe ministry cannot be limited to men also point to Phoebe, a leader in the church in Cenchrea. Paul referred to her as a διακονον of the church, a word most translations render "servant." However, the same translations render the term as "deacon" in 1 Timothy 3. The New Testament often uses this term for ministers or leaders of congregations. In their official position paper on women in ministry, the Assemblies of God says of this term, "It seems likely that *diakonos* was the designation for an official leadership position in the Early Church."[21]

The question must then be asked, what then of the passages that seem to prohibit women from serving as pastors and elders? The two primary passages that specifically withhold this role from women are 1 Corinthians 14:34-35 and 1 Timothy 2:11-15. The requirements for a pastor in 1 Timothy 3 and Titus 1 are, according to this view, neutral regarding gender. The other two passages are not neutral. However, this view sees a way to explain them without surrendering biblical authority or excluding gifted women from ministry.

First Corinthians 14:34 tells women to be silent in the church. However, according to this view, Paul earlier told women to wear something on their heads denoting their submission to authority when they prayed or prophesied before the church (see 1 Corinthians 11:3-10). Both praying publicly and prophesying required women to speak. Either Paul contradicted himself three chapters later, or he had something else in mind in 1 Corinthians 14. Those who hold this view believe that some women must have been disrupting church services by asking questions in the middle of the service or perhaps speaking in tongues at inappropriate times. It may be that Paul was addressing a disruptive group that sat and talked to one another through the service. Therefore, the command to women to stay silent wasn't a blanket statement, but was rather directed toward those who needed to pipe down so the church could conduct its worship services.

First Timothy 2:11-15 also needs to be viewed within the larger context of the New Testament and the historical situation in Ephesus where this letter was addressed. The rest of 1 Timothy suggests there were other problems within the church that centered on a group of women. Paul also told them, "I want women to be modest in their appearance. They should wear decent and appropriate clothing and not draw attention to themselves by the way they fix their hair or by wearing gold or pearls or expensive clothes" (1 Timothy 2:9). Apparently, some women in this church had a habit of dressing immodestly and drawing the wrong kind of attention to themselves. Therefore, according to this view, Paul was addressing a local cultural issue in this chapter, rather than giving a hard-and-fast rule for all churches at all times.

For further support, this position points to Galatians 3:28, which states, "There is no longer Jew or Gentile, slave or free, male or female. For you are all Christians—you are one in Christ Jesus." Just as Christ breaks down barriers created by race, he tears down those built by gender. If this is true, why would God exclude women from serving in some ministry positions within his church? In the same way, if God has called and used women in a variety of leadership positions over his people stretching back to the days of Moses, why would he exclude them today?

As with those who believe the positions of pastors and elders should be filled by men alone, this viewpoint appeals not to changes in culture but to the unchanging Word of God. Which view is correct? Consider the evidence and think for yourself.

What happens when people die?

In the section on Jesus, we explored the question of what will happen when Christ returns. However, the talk of eternal destinies and heaven and hell isn't just confined to eschatology, the study of last things. Each person must also come to grips with a personal eschatology—that is, what is going to happen when your life ends? When Jesus returns, those Christians who are dead will be raised to life, and those who are alive will be immediately transformed into their eternal bodies (see 1 Thessalonians 4:13-18). But what happens in the meantime to those who die? Do we go straight to heaven, and if so, why do our bodies need to be raised back to life? Or do our souls sleep alongside our bodies awaiting Jesus' return? And then there's the question no one really wants to ask. What happens to those who do not know Jesus as their Savior when they die?

Purgatory

Roman Catholics teach that wicked people go directly to hell when they die, while those who are pure go to heaven. However, they believe there is a third option for those who depart this life in a state of God's grace but who have not yet cleansed themselves of all their faults. These people go to a place called purgatory (from the Latin *purgare*, which means to make clean or to purify), where they will be both punished and cleansed of the final traces of sin. "The Catholic doctrine of purgatory supposes the fact that some die with smaller faults for which there was no true repentance, and also the fact that the temporal penalty due to sin is at times not wholly paid in this life."[22] According to Thomas Aquinas, the degree of punishment is based less on the severity of the sin than it is on the disposition of the person punished. "A person who has a better temperament is punished more severely by the same sentence than another; and yet the judge acts justly in condemning both for the same crimes to the same punishment,"[23] he wrote. Only God can know the time each soul must spend in purgatory. However, the prayers of the living on behalf of the dead can help the dead along.

This doctrine seems odd to Protestants. The biggest question they raise is, where in the Bible does the idea come from? Catholics base their belief on both the tradition of the church as well as a passage in the apocryphal book of 2 Maccabees 12:43-46:

> He then took up a collection among all his soldiers, amounting to two thousand silver drachmas, which he sent to Jerusalem to provide for an expiatory sacrifice. In doing this he acted in a very excellent and noble way, inasmuch as he had the resurrection of the dead in view; for if he were not expecting the fallen to rise again, it would have been useless and foolish to pray for them in death. But if he did this with a view to the splendid reward that awaits those who had gone to rest in godliness, it was a holy and pious thought. Thus he made atonement for the dead that they might be freed from this sin.

Catholics reason, if the eternal fate of the dead is set, why would anyone need to pray for them? Therefore, they conclude that further action is needed that "they might be freed from this sin." They also point to 1 Corinthians 3:12-15, which says that our works will be tested by fire. This, adherents of purgatory believe, is part of the purpose of this intermediate state.

Soul Sleep

Soul sleep, also known as psychopannychism (from the Greek words for "soul" and "to last the night"), is the belief that between death and the Second Coming, our souls remain joined with our dead bodies. There they sleep in an unconscious state until the sound of the trumpet signifying Christ's return. When the trumpet sounds, the body arises and the soul awakens, and both are changed into a form that will last for eternity. From the standpoint of the dead, the transformation feels as though it happened at the moment of death, for the soul doesn't dream during this sleep. This view is most closely identified with Seventh-day Adventists.

Supporters of this view include William Tyndale, who wrote in 1530, "And ye, in putting them [the departed souls] in heaven, hell and purgatory, destroy the arguments where-with Christ and Paul prove the resurrection. . . . And again, if the souls be in heaven, tell me why they be not in as good a case as the angels be? And then what cause is there of the resurrection?"[24] Some supporters of this view also quote Martin Luther's commentary on Ecclesiastes and say the reformer believed in soul sleep as well.

Soul sleep proponents point to several passages in the Bible as proof of their position. These include Jesus' comments about Lazarus before he raised him from the dead in John 11:11-14. Jesus told his disciples, "Our friend Lazarus has fallen asleep, but now I will go and wake him up." The disciples assumed Jesus meant physical sleep until Jesus told them plainly, "Lazarus is dead." Other passages refer to death as sleep, including Acts 7:60 and 13:36 (NIV). This view also cites Ecclesiastes 9:10, which says, "For when you go to the grave, there will be no work or planning or knowledge or wisdom," and Job 3:17,

"For in death the wicked cease from troubling, and the weary are at rest."

In response, opponents of this view point to the many passages that speak of consciousness after death and the soul's immediate transportation to either heaven or hell. In Luke 16:19-31, Jesus told the story of the rich man and a beggar named Lazarus (not to be confused with Jesus' friend of the same name). Both men died. The angels carried the beggar to heaven, where he was comforted by Abraham. The rich man went to hell (literally, hades). There he cried out in his agony and begged that someone would be sent to his living brothers to keep them from suffering the same fate as he. Jesus' story presupposes the dead immediately enter into their reward. In the same way, his words to the thief on the cross, "Today you will be with me in paradise" (Luke 23:43), are meaningless if the dead sleep until the Second Coming.

Paul spoke of death as though the soul goes immediately to be with the Lord. In 2 Corinthians 5:6-10 he said:

> So we are always confident, even though we know that as long as we live in these bodies we are not at home with the Lord. That is why we live by believing and not by seeing. Yes, we are fully confident, and we would rather be away from these bodies, for then we will be at home with the Lord. So our aim is to please him always, whether we are here in this body or away from this body. For we must all stand before Christ to be judged. We will each receive whatever we deserve for the good or evil we have done in our bodies.

Critics of soul sleep point out that the phrase "to be absent from the body is to be home with the Lord" leaves little room for the soul sleeping in the body until the final resurrection. The appearance of the souls of the martyrs under God's altar in Revelation 6:9-11 is further proof, critics say, that the idea of soul sleep is in error.

Absent from the Body, at Home with the Lord

Traditionally, Protestants have believed the Bible teaches that when believers die, their souls go to be with the Lord, while unbelievers are separated from him forever in a place of eternal punishment. The vast majority of Protestants reject the idea that there is a third option called purgatory, because it's not explicitly taught in the Bible. As for soul sleep, historically, believers have understood that while the Bible does at times use the word "sleep" for death, the reference is to the body, not the soul.

Paul's words of encouragement to the church in Philippi are a good summary of the hope believers have as they face death. He wrote, "For to me, to live is Christ and to die is gain. If I am to go on living in the body, this will mean fruitful labor for me. Yet what shall I choose? I do not know! I am torn between the two: I desire to depart and be with Christ, which is better by far" (Philippians 1:21-23, NIV). Paul echoed this same sentiment in 2 Corinthians 5:6-10. In both, he expressed the dilemma that all believers face. While life on earth gives us opportunities to be used by God, going home to bask in his presence is much better. We want to join in the heavenly choir pictured in Revelation 4–5 that constantly sings praises to the Lord.

Resurrection Bodies

This still leaves one question unanswered. If we go to be with the Lord immediately after we die, what is the point of our bodies being raised when Christ returns? What possible benefit could this have for us? Paul said Christ will humble all of his enemies under his feet, and the last enemy to be destroyed will be death (see 1 Corinthians 15:25-26). How? God will raise the bodies of his children and clothe them in immortality. If our bodies remain dead, death wins. But Christ conquered death on the cross, and the final results of that victory will spread over us all at the resurrection. Our new resurrection bodies will not die, nor will they suffer any of the effects of sin or the weakness we face now (see 1 Corinthians 15:42-44). How closely our new bodies will resemble our current bodies the Bible does not say. However, Jesus looked essentially the same after he rose from the dead. He even carried the scars from the nail and spear wounds he received when he was crucified.

The fact the Jesus will raise our physical bodies and clothe them with glory when he returns emphasizes how important bodies are. We aren't souls that temporarily inhabit bodies. We are people who will have bodies eternally. Our earthly tent, as 2 Corinthians 4 describes the body, may be weak, but it was still made to glorify God. As we saw in the chapter on the Holy Spirit, the Bible calls the believer's body a "temple of the Holy Spirit." Paul said God bought us with a high price, so we must glorify God with our bodies (see 1 Corinthians 6:19-20). He urged his readers to run away from sexual sin, for it is a sin against our own bodies. Again, in God's eyes, how we use our bodies matters more than we can comprehend. He made them to glorify him, which is how we must now use them.

Hell

Those who die without Christ will be separated from God forever in a place called hell. God made hell as an eternal punishment for the Devil and his demons (see Matthew 25:41).

Jesus described hell as a place where the worm never dies and the fire is never quenched (see Mark 9:48). In the story of the rich man and Lazarus, the rich man was so tormented that he would have been satisfied to have just a drop of water touch his tongue (see Luke 16:24). While most people use the word *hell* flippantly, the Bible paints a gruesome picture of this place of torment. The knowledge that hell is real and that people will end up there without Jesus should motivate us to tell more people about Christ. William Carey, the father of modern missions, used to weep over a globe as he thought about the millions of people who had never even heard of Jesus, much less had the opportunity to believe in him.

The horrors of hell have led many people to look for a different option. One is called annihilationism, which teaches that the souls of the wicked are burned up to the point that they cease to exist. This view is mostly held by Adventist groups, as well as the non-Christian group Jehovah's Witnesses. Others mitigate the horrors of hell with the belief that eventually everyone will be allowed to enter heaven. This is known as universalism, or the belief that God will save everyone. Universalism is not a mainstream Christian idea. Most if not all universalists reject key truths of the Bible, including the Trinity and the deity of Christ. However, some people claim to be both evangelical Christians and universalists. One such person defends the belief by saying, "It's the only way I can sleep at night." Unfortunately, ignoring truth doesn't make it any less true.

The doctrine of hell should be distasteful for all of us. It is to God. That's why God sent his Son. John said, "God did not send his Son into the world to condemn it, but to save it" (John 3:17). Salvation means more than being delivered from hell, but it's a big part of it. Throughout the Bible we see

God pleading with people to be reconciled to him. The book of Jonah shows how eager he is to grant mercy to anyone who will receive it. But that's the problem that makes hell inevitable. Not everyone wants God's mercy. C. S. Lewis put it this way:

> In the long run the answer to all those who object to the doctrine of hell is itself a question: "What are you asking God to do?" To wipe out their past sins and, at all costs, to give them a fresh start, smoothing every difficulty and offering every miraculous help? But He has done so, on Calvary. To forgive them? They will not be forgiven. To leave them alone? Alas, I am afraid that it is what He does.[25]

Several years ago I conducted a funeral for a man who had alienated almost everyone in his family. None of his sons would talk to me about their father, for he had spent most of his life making all of them miserable. He was an angry, bitter old man who took out his anger on everyone around him. When it came to God and the Bible, the man's attitude was pretty much the same. He didn't care for either.

After the funeral a little boy came up to me and asked, "Is my grandpa in heaven?" I don't know where my response came from, except to say it came from the Holy Spirit. I simply told the little boy, "Your grandpa is in God's hands now, and he will do what is right." At the end of the day, this is what our understanding of hell comes down to. The God we love and trust will always do what is right. This is what allows me to sleep at night.

Epilogue

Where Do You Go from Here?

The single most popular question in schools today is rarely asked out loud: "So when are we ever going to use this in the real world?" As you sit in front of a textbook memorizing some obscure algebraic formula, you ask it. When you are forced to read a few hundred pages on the first and second Punic Wars, you ask it. When you try to force yourself to pay attention while your instructor waxes eloquent about the difference between gerunds, participles, and infinitives, you ask it. "When am I ever going to use *this*?"

After wading through this book, you may be asking yourself the same thing. "So how am I going to use my beliefs about the Trinity in the real world?" You are already living your answer, whether you realize it or not. Your life has already been shaped by what you believe about the subjects we just explored. The process is far from over. As you travel through life, you will face many decisions. Your beliefs will determine which paths you take. In those moments, all your talk about God and faith will be put to the test. Your real beliefs, those that remain when everything else is stripped away, will reveal themselves.

That's how you will use what you've just read in the real world. And that's why this book is only the beginning. There's not just a world to explore lying before you. As a Christ follower, an even greater quest awaits you. You have a God to get to know. The Westminster Catechism says your highest purpose for being alive is to know God and enjoy him forever. Knowing God means growing in your understanding of theology. It will take you deeper into all the subjects we covered so briefly here.

No matter how long you live, there will still be new facets of God to discover.

Moreover, this God who wants to know you has charted a course he wants to take you down. Many people think finding God's path for their lives involves nothing more than asking for his guidance on the big questions, such as what career path they should take and who they should marry. That only scratches the surface. The Lord wants you to experience life his way. When you do, get ready for some surprises. Along the way you will discover truths about him that will blow your mind. You will also encounter tests of your faith that will threaten to turn everything you ever thought you knew upside down. Everything you encounter as you walk with God has a purpose. We tend to focus on arriving at some destination, whether it be success or marriage or the ultimate destination: heaven itself. But God looks at our lives as a whole. He cares just as much about the journey as he does the destinations. His goal is to remake you along the way while also touching the lives of others through your life.

Your beliefs are also a journey rather than a final destination. This doesn't mean they will change completely from week to week or year to year. Instead, you need to see yourself as a lifelong learner with God and view his Word as your teacher. The goal isn't just to accumulate knowledge, but to come to know God better every day. This is what keeps your relationship with him fresh. Too many people cram a handful of beliefs about God in their pocket and think they are set for life. They treat God like the stereotypical tough guy treats his wife: the guy who tells her he loves her on their wedding day and thinks that should be sufficient for the rest of their lives. Knowing God means falling more in love with him as you learn more of him and the way he works in the world.

All of this brings us to the question: Where do you go from here? If this book is merely the starting point on a lifelong journey into God, what step do you take next?

Read

Paul said faith comes by hearing the message of good news (see Romans 10:17). If your faith is going to grow, you need to hear more and more of this message of good news. The simplest way to do this is to read. Paul wrote, "Let the words of Christ, in all their richness, live in your hearts and make you wise" (Colossians 3:16). The best way to open your life to the words of Christ in all their richness is to read them over and over again. Don't just read selected passages you grab from here and there across the Bible. Read all of God's Word from beginning to end.

If you don't know where to start, get a copy of a one-year Bible, such as *The Message REMIX: Pause*. Start on day one and read. Every day you will read part of both the Old and New Testaments. If you need help understanding some of the difficult parts or with making sense of the Bible's big picture, grab a copy of a book such as *The Bible: Think for Yourself About What's Inside*. Whatever you decide, the most important thing you can do is to read the Bible for yourself. You will be amazed at how God will change your mind, your heart, and your life as you do.

Once you start reading the Bible, keep reading. Read books that challenge you to think. Believers have written about their encounters with God for more than two thousand years. Learn from their insights. Read a variety of works from believers across both time and theological perspectives. Many classic works can be found online for free at www.ccel.org. These include devotional classics such as Thomas à Kempis's *The Imitation of Christ*, as well as deeper theological masterpieces such as the works of Jonathan Edwards and Augustine. You will also find both books and sermons by men such as John Wesley, who shaped the beliefs of many churches in America today. Many valuable books by recent authors are available as well.

Think

As you read, think through the ideas you encounter. Ask questions and take the concepts presented to their logical conclusion. Compare new ideas to the essentials of the faith. And always let the Bible be the ultimate judge of everything you read. Many people cite verses as proof of what they say. Read the Bible for yourself and let it be the judge of whether or not the proof texts are being used properly. Remember, the Devil quoted the Bible when he tempted Jesus. Just because someone says, "The Bible says . . ." doesn't make it so.

Thinking through your beliefs also opens the door for discussions with other believers. Proverbs 27:17 says that just as iron sharpens iron, we are to sharpen one another. If you've ever sharpened a knife, you know the process includes friction and sparks. The same will be true as you discuss questions with brothers and sisters in Christ with whom you don't see eye to eye. Rather than allow your differences to divide you, let them become a means by which God sharpens you both. Remember the words of Romans 14:1:

> Welcome with open arms fellow believers who don't see things the way you do. And don't jump all over them every time they do or say something you don't agree with — even when it seems that they are strong on opinions but weak

in the faith department. Remember, they have their own history to deal with. Treat them gently. (MSG)

God's family includes people with many different perspectives. Let these different perspectives sharpen you as you listen and think.

Pray

The purpose of theology is to allow you to know God. At times we confuse knowing God with knowing facts about him. The facts are only half of the equation. As you come face-to-face with the glorious truths God reveals about himself, you should adore him and love him more. Truly learning theology will leave you in prayer and worship. Allow God's truth to not only fill your head, but to also permeate your heart.

Perhaps the greatest American theologian was an eighteenth-century pastor named Jonathan Edwards. Many people know of him only because of a sermon he wrote called "Sinners in the Hands of an Angry God." Because of this, they think Edwards was the typical fire-and-brimstone preacher who tried to scare people into believing in Jesus. Yet Edwards was much more. He had an incredible grasp on the wonder of knowing God. He wrote, "It is easily proved that the highest end and happiness of man is to *view God's excellency*, to *love* him, and *receive expressions* of his love."[1] This is where this journey into theology should lead you.

Live

All of our talk about God ultimately comes down to this: Are we living it? As you walk with and learn from God, you must put your theology into practice. James said faith without works is dead. The same is true of your theology. Any belief system that doesn't express itself in a life that imitates Jesus' life is worthless. As Matthew 25:31-46 makes clear, it isn't what we *say* we believe that matters, but how we *live* what we believe that makes all the difference.

Notes

Introduction

1. "Positive Atheism's Big List of Quotations," http://www.positiveatheism
   .org/hist/quotes/quote-t.htm.

2. G. K. Chesterton, *Heretics* (New York: John Lane Company, 1908),
   CCEL.org e-edition, 7.

3. The American Kennel Club officially recognizes 158 breeds. However,
   when you throw in mixed-breed dogs, along with customized breeds
   such as the Labradoodle (half Lab, half poodle), the number jumps
   considerably.

Section One

1. Max Tegmark, "Parallel Universes," *Science and Ultimate Reality:
   Quantum Theory, Cosmology, and Complexity*, eds. J. D. Barrow, P. C.
   W. Davies, and C. L. Harper Jr. (Cambridge: Cambridge University
   Press, 2004), 470–471.

2. Go to http://hubblesite.org/gallery for photographs of the universe
   that must be seen to be believed.

3. For more, go to his website, http://space.mit.edu/home/tegmark/
   index.html, or check out his article "Parallel Universes," in the May
   2003 issue of *Scientific American* at www.sciam.com/article.cfm
   ?chanID=sa006&articleID=000F1EDD-B48A-1E90
   -8EA5809EC5880000.

4. Barbara W. Tuchman, *The Guns of August* (New York: Macmillan,
   1962), 21.

5. This, in part, explains why Rick Warren's book *The Purpose Driven
   Life* has sold over 20 million copies in hardcover.

6. Francis Schaeffer, *How Should We Then Live?* (Downers Grove, IL:
   Crossway, 1976), 159.

7. C. S. Lewis, *Mere Christianity* (San Francisco: HarperSanFrancisco,
   1952; New York: HarperCollins, 2001), 4. Citations are to the
   HarperCollins edition.

8. Millard J. Erickson, *Christian Theology, Vol. 1* (Grand Rapids, MI: Baker, 1983), 175.

9. Erickson, 191.

10. "Inspiration," *The International Standard Bible Encyclopedia*, www.studylight.org/enc/isb.

11. Roman Catholic Bibles do contain additional books or additions to existing books in the Old Testament known as the Apocrypha, which Protestants do not consider Scripture. These include Tobit, Judith, Wisdom, Ecclesiasticus, Baruch, 1 and 2 Maccabees, and certain supplementary parts of Esther and Daniel. Although a few doctrines upon which Catholics and Protestants disagree have their roots in these books, overall their presence does not radically alter the core doctrines upon which Christianity rests.

12. David Ewert, *From Ancient Tablets to Modern Translations: A General Introduction to the Bible* (Grand Rapids, MI: Zondervan, 1983), 189.

13. Ewert, 202.

14. C. S. Lewis, "Modern Translations of the Bible," *God in the Dock* (Grand Rapids, MI: Eerdmans, 1970), 230–231.

15. Erickson, 233–234, emphasis added.

16. Erickson, 222–223.

17. See Brian McLaren, "Soft on Scripture?" www.anewkindofchristian .com/archives/000154.html.

18. This is why the Declaration of Independence says, "We hold these Truths to be self-evident . . ."

19. For a fuller explanation, see Stanley J. Grenz and John R. Franke, *Beyond Foundationalism: Shaping Theology in a Postmodern Context*, especially chapter 3, "Scripture: Theology's Norming Norm" (Louisville, KY: Westminster John Knox Press, 2001).

20. Grenz and Franke, 63.

21. Robert Webber, *The Younger Evangelicals: Facing the Challenges of the New World* (Grand Rapids, MI: Baker, 2002), 99.

Section Two

1. John Calvin, *Institutes of the Christian Religion*, Book First, Chapter V, Section 9, trans. Henry Beveridge (Grand Rapids, MI: Eerdmans, 1989), 57.

2. Jonathan Edwards, "Miscellaneous Observations on Important Theological Subjects," *The Complete Works of Jonathan Edwards, Vol. 2* (1834; repr., Carlisle, PA: The Banner of Truth Trust, 1995), 1139.

3. For a full discussion of the difference between the God of the Bible and the gods of other worldviews, see *Worldviews: Think for Yourself About How You See God*, part of the TH1NK REFERENCE COLLECTION.

4. You can read selected chapters in The Message and other translations at www.biblegateway.com.

5. C. S. Lewis, *Mere Christianity* (San Francisco: HarperSanFrancisco, 1952; New York: HarperCollins, 2001), 163. Citations are to the HarperCollins edition.

6. Lewis, 161.

7. Millard J. Erickson, *Christian Theology, Vol. 1* (Grand Rapids, MI: Baker, 1983), 342.

8. For a more complete discussion of naturalism, see *Worldviews: Think for Yourself About How You See God*.

9. Intelligent Design Theory is not included in this discussion because, although it is championed primarily by Christians, it falls outside the scope of this book. Rather than offering specific answers to the questions we explore in this chapter, the theory simply says that the universe shows evidence of a Creator without specifically identifying that Creator as the God of the Bible.

10. Kurt Wise, *Faith, Form, and Time: What the Bible Teaches and Science Confirms About Creation and the Age of the Universe* (Nashville: Broadman, Holman, 2002), 57, emphasis added.

11. Erickson, 383.

12. "C. S. Lewis on Creation and Evolution: The Acworth Letters, 1944–1960," *Perspectives on Science and Christian Faith*, vol. 48, no. 1 (March 1996): 3, www.apologetics.org/acworthletters3.html.

13. For more, see Ken Matthews, *The New American Commentary, Genesis 1–11:26* (Nashville: Broadman, Holman, 1996), 108.

14. Francis A. Schaeffer, *Genesis in Space and Time*, from *The Complete Works of Francis Schaeffer, Vol. 2, A Christian View of the Bible as Truth* (Westchester, IL: Crossway, 1982), 39.

15. Wise, 89.

16. Charles Colson and Nancy Pearcey, *How Now Shall We Live?* (Wheaton, IL: Tyndale, 1999), 61.

17. Epicurus, *Aphorisms*, quoted in James A. Haught, *2000 Years of Disbelief: Famous People with the Courage to Doubt* (Amherst, NY: Prometheus Books, 2000), 19.

18. Mark Tabb, *Greater Than: Unconventional Thoughts on the Infinite God* (Colorado Springs, CO: NavPress, 2005), 99.

19. George MacDonald, *Unspoken Sermons, Series One*, quoted in C. S. Lewis, *The Problem of Pain*, paperback ed. (New York: Collier Books, Macmillan, 1962), 7.

20. This has been, to be sure, a very short treatment of the subject of pain that was never meant to be comprehensive. For further study, read C. S. Lewis's *The Problem of Pain* or Mark Tabb's *Out of the Whirlwind*.

21. For a full discussion, see Calvin's *Institutes*, Book Second, Chapter II.

Section Three

1. Various photographs of the Alexamenos Graffito can be found on the Web at http://faculty.bbc.edu/rdecker/alex_graffito.htm and http://penelope.uchicago.edu/~grout/encyclopaedia_romana/gladiators/graffito.html. The donkey head on the figure on the cross was probably meant as a slap at the Jewish roots of Christianity. Ancient critics charged Jews with worshiping an ass, supposedly because a herd of asses led them out of the wilderness after they left Egypt.

2. Jehovah's Witnesses do this in their New World Translation.

3. John R. W. Stott, *The Cross of Christ* (Downers Grove, IL: InterVarsity, 1986), 68.

4. The ancient Israelites were divided into twelve tribes based on their descent from Jacob's twelve sons. These were Reuben, Simeon, Levi, Judah, Issachar, Zebulun, Gad, Asher, Joseph, Benjamin, Dan, and Naphtali.

Section Four

1. J. I. Packer, *Keep in Step with the Spirit* (Old Tappan, NJ: Revell, 1984), 49.

2. Packer, 66.

3. John Wesley, "On Patience," *Sermons on Several Occasions*, Christian Classics Ethereal Library: Grand Rapids, MI, public domain, originally published in 1771, www.ccel.org/ccel/wesley/sermons.vi.xxx.htm.

4. Millard J. Erickson, *Christian Theology, Vol. 1* (Grand Rapids, MI: Baker, 1983), 970.

5. *Charismatic* comes from the Greek word for spiritual gift used in 1 Corinthians 12 and 14, *charis*. *Pentecostal* refers to the pouring out of the Spirit on the day of Pentecost in Acts 2.

6. W. A. Criswell, "The Baptism of the Holy Spirit" sermon preached February 6, 1977, at the First Baptist Church, Dallas, TX, www.wacriswell.com/index.cfm/FuseAction/Search.Transcripts/sermon/109.cfm.

7. Francis A. Schaeffer, *True Spirituality* (Wheaton, IL: Tyndale, 1982), 76.

8. Erickson, 879–880.

9. The General Council of the Assemblies of God, "The Baptism in the Holy Spirit: The Initial Experience and Continuing Evidences of the Spirit-Filled Life," official A/G position paper, adopted August 11, 2000, http://ag.org/top/Beliefs/Position_Papers/pp_4185_spirit-filled_life.cfm.

10. However, unlike Acts 2, the tongues spoken by most modern charismatics and Pentecostals are not known human languages. Adherents

point to 1 Corinthians 13:1 (NIV), which refers to "tongues of angels," as evidence that the language spoken in tongues is not of this world.

11. The General Council of the Assemblies of God, "The Baptism in the Holy Spirit: The Initial Experience and Continuing Evidences of the Spirit-Filled Life."

12. The Gospels record two instances where Jesus fed large crowds. He fed five thousand with five loaves and two fish (Matthew 14:13-21; Mark 6:32-44; Luke 9:10-17; John 6:1-13), and he fed four thousand with seven loaves and a few small fish (Matthew 15:32-39; Mark 8:1-10).

13. The General Council of the Assemblies of God, "Diving Healing: An Integral Part of the Gospel," official A/G position paper, http://ag.org/top/Beliefs/Position_Papers/pp_4184_healing.cfm.

14. C. S. Lewis, *Miracles* (New York: Macmillan, 1947, 1960), 167.

15. Mary Crawford, *The Shantung Revival* (Shanghai: China Baptist Publication Society, 1933).

Section Five

1. Rick Warren, *The Purpose Driven Life* (Grand Rapids, MI: Zondervan, 2002), 19.

2. Stanley J. Grenz and John R. Franke, *Beyond Foundationalism: Shaping Theology in a Postmodern Context* (Louisville, KY: Westminster John Knox Press, 2001), 228.

3. The book of Hosea paints the best picture of this relationship.

4. Millard J. Erickson, *Christian Theology, Vol. 1* (Grand Rapids, MI: Baker, 1983), 994.

5. Free Methodist Church, "Articles of Religion: Salvation, XIII: Restoration," http://www.freemethodistchurch.org/Sections/About%20Us/Beliefs/Doctrines/Articles%2010-13.htm.

6. Thomas C. Oden, *John Wesley's Scriptural Christianity* (Grand Rapids, MI: Zondervan, 1994), 243.

7. James Arminius, *Works of J. Arminius, Vol. 1*, www.ccel.org/ccel/arminius/works1.iii.vii.html.

8. John Wesley, "On Faith," *Sermons on Several Occasions*, www.ccel.org/ccel/wesley/sermons.vii.xiv.html.

9. John Wesley, "A Call to Backsliders," *Sermons on Several Occasions*, www.ccel.org/ccel/wesley/sermons.vi.xxxiii.html.

10. "The Decree for the Armenians," in the Bull "Exultate Deo" of Pope Eugene IV, http://www.newadvent.org/cathen/02258b.htm.

11. Augustine, "Why the Children of the Baptized Should Be Baptized," *Anti-Pelagian Writings*, www.ccel.org/ccel/schaff/npnf105.x.iv.xliii.html.

12. Martin Luther, *Luther's Little Instruction Book: The Small Catechism of Martin Luther*, trans. Robert E. Smith (Fort Wayne, IN: Project Wittenberg, 2002), from the German text, printed in *Triglot Concordia: The Symbolical Books of the Ev. Lutheran Church* (St. Louis: Concordia, 1921), 538–559.

13. Erickson, 1092.

14. G. R. Beasly Murray, "Baptism," *The New International Dictionary of New Testament Theology, Vol. 1*, ed. Colin Brown (Grand Rapids, MI: Zondervan, 1975), 144.

15. Paul Johnson, *A History of the American People* (New York: HarperCollins, 1997), 33.

16. Ronald Reagan, "Farewell Address to the Nation," January 11, 1989, http://www.ronaldreagan.com/sp_21.html.

17. Charles Colson's book *Kingdoms in Conflict* is a must-read for those who want to understand the role of believers within the state.

18. John W. Whitehead, "Churches and the Corrupting Influence of Politics," July 26, 2004, The Rutherford Institute, www.rutherford.org/articles_db/commentary.asp?record_id=292.

19. Dorothy Patterson, "Women, The Baptist Faith and Message and Charles Stanley," December 15, 2004, article appearing on the Council of Biblical Manhood and Womanhood, www.cbmw.org/article.php?id=104.

20. The Executive Committee of the Southern Baptist Convention, "Southern Baptists and Women Pastors," 2006, www.baptist2baptist .net/printfriendly.asp?ID=58.

21. The General Council of the Assemblies of God, "The Role of Women in Ministry," official A/G position paper, http://ag.org/top/Beliefs/ Position_Papers/pp_4191_women_ministry.cfm.

22. Edward J. Hanna, "Purgatory," *The Catholic Encyclopedia, Vol. XII* (New York: Robert Appleton Company, 1911), online edition by K. Knight, 2003, www.newadvent.org/cathen/12575a.htm.

23. Thomas Aquinas, "Summa Theologica," www.ccel.org/ccel/aquinas/ summa.AP1_Q2_A1.html.

24. William Tyndale, *An Answer to Sir Thomas More's Dialogue* (Parker's 1850 reprint), bk. 4, ch. 4, 180–181.

25. C. S. Lewis, *The Problem of Pain* (New York: Macmillan, 1962), 128.

Epilogue

1. Jonathan Edwards, "Miscellaneous Observations on Important Theological Subjects," *The Complete Works of Jonathan Edwards, Vol. 2* (1834; repr., Carlisle, PA: The Banner of Truth Trust, 1995), 1139.

About the Author

MARK TABB is general editor of the TH1NK REFERENCE COLLECTION, as well as the author of twelve books, including *Living with Less* and *Greater Than: Unconventional Thoughts on the Infinite God*. He and his family live in Indiana with their two dachshunds.

About the Scholar Board

All books in the TH1NK REFERENCE COLLECTION have been reviewed for biblical accuracy by the following academic scholars:

Robert Don Hughes, PhD
professor of missions and evangelism, Clear Creek Baptist College, Pineville, Kentucky

Bob has a strong pastoral background as well as great strength as a writer. He knows people. He knows their needs. He is on this board to make sure these books speak to real people in the real world. In addition, he has impeccable academic qualifications and understands and works well with those from across the theological scale.

Jerry A. Johnson, PhD
president and professor of theology and ethics, The Criswell College, Dallas, Texas

Jerry has extensive expertise in the area of theology and worldviews. In addition to serving as president of The Criswell College and as a theology professor there, he has a daily radio program that focuses on applying a Christian worldview to every aspect of life.

Keith Reeves, PhD
professor of New Testament and early Christian literature in the School of Theology, Azusa Pacific University, Azusa, California

Keith brings a different perspective to the books, from both a theological and geographical standpoint. His views on the Bible and creation differ from the others on the scholar board. Also, the fact that he teaches in Southern California gives him a different perspective from both the writers of the first three books and the members of the board. In addition, Keith is an expert in New Testament and early Christian literature.

Joseph Thomas, PhD
assistant professor of church history, Biblical Seminary, Hatfield, Pennsylvania; director of Christian History Institute (CHI)

Joe combines a strong background in church history with a Wesleyan/Holiness theological background. Before pursuing his PhD, he taught history in a Christian high school for eight years, thereby developing a strong ability to communicate with our target audience.

GET THE FULL THINK STUDENT LIBRARY.

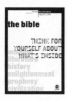

The Bible
1-57683-956-7
This easy-to-understand guide to the Bible will provide valuable insights and answers to the tough questions while leading students through God's Word.

Worldviews
1-57683-955-9
Worldviews is a quick-reference tool that equips students with a broad perspective on the various world beliefs and religions while comparing them to the Christian faith.